The Pattern of Hardy's Poetry

The Pattern of Hardy's Poetry

BY

SAMUEL HYNES

Chapel Hill

THE UNIVERSITY OF NORTH CAROLINA PRESS

1961

Copyright © 1956 by
Samuel Hynes
Manufactured in the United States of America

PRINTED BY THE SEEMAN PRINTERY, DURHAM, N. C.

THIS BOOK WAS DIGITALLY PRINTED.

For my Father

Preface

THIS STUDY OF Hardy's poetry is organized, as the title suggests, around a single, simple assertion—that there is a pattern in the poetry, a pattern having both philosophical and poetic aspects, and that by discovering and examining this pattern we can come to a proper understanding of the poems. The pattern that I find in Hardy is not an intricate one—no Jamesian figure in the carpet—but simply the eternal conflict between irreconcilables, which was for Hardy the first principle, and indeed the only principle, of universal order. This idea of eternal conflict is manifested not only in the philosophical content of Hardy's poems, but also in their structure, diction, and imagery—it gives form to every aspect of substance and technique.

The principal intention of this book is to define and explain the ways in which the pattern of Hardy's poetry works; I have therefore arranged the central section of the book (Chapters 3-7) into separate discussions of Hardy's philosophy, style, forms, diction, etc. I have found it necessary, however, to preface these analyses with two introductory chapters which treat Hardy's reputation and some of the reasons for it; and in the last three chapters I have drawn some conclusions about Hardy's development, and about the nature of his achievement.

It may seem to some readers that I have over-emphasized Hardy's weaknesses as a poet, and under-emphasized his strengths. Certainly I have taken that "full look at the Worst" that Hardy prescribed; but I have done so in order to establish the peculiar, personal qualities of Hardy's very considerable successes. In Hardy's work, more perhaps than in the work of most poets, good poems and bad poems resemble each other, rather as the family beauty resembles the ugly duckling—you can see the same bone-structure, even though the flesh is arranged differently. Frequently a bad poem has seemed to offer a better example than a good poem would, simply because its bone-structure *is* so clear, its "pattern" so overt: I have tried to maintain a reasonable balance by also including analyses of a number of the poems which I consider Hardy's best. But in the end, this book is not about either the good or the bad poems—it is about all the poems.

I have been helped in this enterprise by a number of persons, and I should like to thank them here. Professors Jerome Buckley, W. Y. Tindall, and Lionel Trilling, of Columbia University, all read an early and considerably different version, and improved it by their comments. My colleagues, Bruce Dearing and Mrs. Elizabeth Wright, also made a number of valuable suggestions. Monroe Beardsley, who for a long time now has been both my friend and my critical conscience, read the most recent draft, and gave me criticism and encouragement when I needed both. And my wife has been steadily sympathetic and tolerant.

Chapter II, in a somewhat different form, appeared in *The South Atlantic Quarterly,* Winter, 1959, and is included here by permission of the editors. Quotations from Hardy's poems and *The Dynasts* are with the permission of the copyright holders, The Macmillan Company and Macmillan and Co., Ltd., and the Trustees of the Hardy Estate; those from *The Early Life of Thomas Hardy* and *The Later Years of Thomas Hardy* are courtesy of the estate of Florence Emily Hardy; *Life and Art* is quoted with the permission of the Chilton Company, the copyright holders. A grant from the Swarthmore College Faculty Research Fund paid for secretarial assistance. I should also like to thank the Ford Foundation for a grant extended through its program for assisting American university presses in the publication of works in the humanities and the social sciences.

Contents

1. Hardy and the Critics — 3
2. Hardy and the Poets — 16
3. The Uses of Philosophy — 34
4. The Hardy Style — 56
5. The Search for a Form — 74
6. The Uses of Diction — 89
7. The Two Worlds of Imagery — 109
8. The Question of Development — 130
9. *The Dynasts* as an Example — 152
10. The Final Achievement — 175
    References — 183
    Notes — 184
    Index — 191

The Pattern of Hardy's Poetry

1

Hardy and the Critics

"THE TROUBLE with Hardy," a man I know once remarked, "is that he is nobody's favorite poet." By this he meant, I think, that great poets need great partisans of their poetry, and that what comes in the end to be the common, public evaluation of the poetry may originate in, or at least be influenced by, the partisanship. At some point in his career the poet needs enthusiastic admiration, true-believers to enunciate and formulate his virtues. Although Hardy came to the conclusion that "a poet may be much injured by over-criticism, that too much commenting and prying into motives, etc., rub the bloom off the poetry,"[1] one might argue instead that criticism rubs the bloom *on,* and poems, like furniture, gain a patina from much handling. Hardy's poetry has not acquired a patina, for so far it has attracted few passionate admirers.

And so, while he seems to occupy a secure position in the hierarchy of English poets, and is in the anthologies and the textbooks, the reasons for his being there remain undefined. Most critics would, I am sure, say that of course they take Hardy's poetry seriously; but in fact few have taken it seriously enough to write about it.

The difficulties which lie in the way of liking Hardy

are numerous, and are both in the verse and outside it. The greatest obstruction is the sheer bulk of poetry which one *cannot* like. Hardy probably wrote more—surely he preserved more—bad poems than any other important poet of our time. While Mrs. Hardy assures us that he destroyed "those he thought irremediably bad," we must disagree with his afterthought that he had destroyed too many. He was apparently a poem-saver as other men are string-savers, and to the end of his life he drew upon his hoard to flesh out his volumes (there are two poems in the posthumous *Winter Words* dated in the 1860's).

To this initial obstruction one may add Hardy's severely limited range of tone and ideas. One comes from reading Hardy's nine-hundred-odd poems with a sense of a single, unvarying tone—nostalgic, ironic, pessimistic—a tone in its way moving and effective in individual poems, but at the same time severely restrictive and, in the end, monotonous. There are, to be sure, poems which are gay and humorous, but they are too few to affect one's general impression. The poetry lacks the enrichment of various tones, and one can no more respond to it in quantity than one can to a single musical note continuously repeated.

Tone and ideas may be regarded as functions of each other: given one, the other follows. In Hardy's case, they are mutually restrictive. Hardy had a few obsessive ideas that determined both the substance and the style of his poems: infidelities of all possible kinds, the inevitable loss of love, the destructiveness of time, the implacable indifference of nature, the cruelty of men, the irreversible pastness of the past. These obsessive ideas are all suitable to the limited tonal range that Hardy employs, and in fact together they virtually exhaust the possibilities of that tone. One can scarcely object to the use of such ideas—they are among the inherited materials of poetry—but when they become obsessive the result may be, and often is in Hardy, a violation of the integrity of the individual poem.

The combination of ironic tone and obsessive ideas in Hardy's poems determines what critics choose to call his "philosophy." It is significant of Hardy's oddness that this philosophy has been the subject of more critical concern than his poetry *as poetry*; probably no other modern poet has been examined so persistently as a thinker.[2] This may be true in part because critics find it easier to talk about ideas than about poems; but it is also true that in some poems a system of thought seems to operate as an extrinsic discipline, forcing the material in the direction of didacticism, or obscuring or replacing the particularity of detail which is one of Hardy's poetic strengths. "Crass Casualty obstructs the sun and rain," Hardy says in an early poem, and this is as descriptive of a part of his poetic practice as it is of the world he saw: his abstractions sometimes get in the way of his things.

Such "philosophical" poems constitute a relatively small part of Hardy's total poetic production, but because they fail so flamboyantly, because they do so little what one expects poems to do, they may seem to bulk larger than they actually do. In a reader radically antagonistic to Hardy's thought, such "idea" poems may create a kind of astigmatism, which will throw even the least philosophical poems out of focus, and thus the philosophy may be an obstruction even where it does not exist.

At the opposite extreme are the poems of small occasions.

They are more frequent, if perhaps less noticeable, than the philosophical failures; they are the flat, anecdotal poems which for one reason or another do not rise above a low level of verse—unobjectionable, but uninteresting. In them Hardy shows something of the relentlessly anecdotal quality of country conversation, in which all events are worth chewing over, and none is too dull to repeat. Hardy's notebooks[3] are full of Dorset gossip of dead lovers and bastards and wronged maidens, and out of this gossip he made poems. At best these poems have the eternal significance of folk ballads—the gossip becomes cosmic gossip—but at worst, and there is more of the worst than of the best in Hardy, they remain merely anecdotes. Apparently Hardy was content that they should remain so. When someone criticized his absurd poem, "In the Days of Crinoline," Hardy replied, "Oh, but it is a true story."[4] Where the critical standard is simply fidelity to facts, the poetic performance is not likely to be high.

Hardy's other technical weaknesses are generally recognized, and have been frequently criticized; they need not be discussed at any length here (though we will return to them later). His language is, as many critics have remarked, odd and quirkish and often uncouth. His command of English metrics is often faulty—in many poems the use of one meter rather than another seems adventitious, and often the meter chosen is patently unsuitable to the material. Meter and rhyme often seem to determine the sense of a line, and even the direction of an entire poem.

Hardy's powers of self-criticism were weak, and he was often guilty of gaucheness, banality, or inadvertent humor which a lesser but more self-conscious poet would have avoided. This weakness led him to mar his *Collected Poems* with many flat and tasteless pieces, which affect our sense of the poetic level of the entire performance. The fact that he did not discard a single poem from his earlier volumes in making up the 1925 collection is significant; Hardy was to the end inflexibly himself: not a poet's poet, nor a critic's poet, but simply his own poet.

Perhaps another reason for Hardy's failure to attract passionate partisans lies in his personality, or rather in the persona which he projected through his verse and prose writings. For while in critical principle we may distinguish meticulously between the poet and the poem, in the less rigorous act of reading and liking a poem we do not always do so. Where poems seem to express a personality (and they are not often as depersonalized as Mr. Eliot would wish), we respond to that personality, and that response in turn colors, and perhaps even determines, our judgment.

The only Hardy that we know, the public persona of his work, is not a man with whom it is easy to involve oneself, in the way that some readers (and critics) find it possible to get involved with, for example, D. H. Lawrence. Hardy did not indulge in self-revelation or confession; he veiled his innermost self in an impenetrable decorum more suitable, one might think, to a cabinet minister or an archbishop than to a poet. He was extremely, almost compulsively, reticent; the device of the autobiography once-removed which he employed in the *Early Life* and the *Later Years* is only one example of this compulsion at work. By using his second wife (apparently a model of decorum herself) as a filtering intelligence, he was able to reduce his own history to a recording of business negotiations, anecdotes, social events, random musings, and bits of descriptive detail, interesting because they are all we have, but neither revealing nor intimate. The inner details—his private feelings about people and books, his aspirations, his triumphs and defeats, his despairs and exultations—are discreetly omitted.

Nor are there any extant letters of a personal nature—apparently Hardy never wrote any, and in fact there is no evidence that he had any friends, except perhaps Horace Moule (who died in 1873) close enough to address confidences to, had he been capable of writing them. After Hardy's death his executor, Sir Sydney Cockerell, went through the correspondence, but concluded that it was not worth publishing. The recent volume of letters collected and edited by Carl J. Weber supports Sir Sydney's opinion.

The poems, even when they are apparently most subjective, are reticent in something like the same way; they are protected from intimacy by irony and understatement and often by various devices of dramatic distance as well. This is perhaps one reason for Hardy's fondness for poems with a plot, and for ballads. Such reticence is not, of course, necessarily a poetic weakness; it may be a considerable strength, as it is in the following excellent poem, "A Night in November":

> I marked when the weather changed,
> And the panes began to quake,
> And the winds rose up and ranged,
> That night, lying half-awake.
>
> Dead leaves blew into my room,
> And alighted upon my bed,
> And a tree declared to the gloom
> Its sorrow that they were shed.

> One leaf of them touched my hand,
> And I thought that it was you
> There stood as you used to stand,
> And saying at last you knew!
>
> (?) 1913.
>
> (*Collected Poems*, p. 555)*

Although this is a first-person poem, it is not in any overt sense a personal one. A reader familiar with Hardy's life might notice the tentative date, and associate the poem with the 1912-13 elegies, and the "you" of the poem with the first Mrs. Hardy, but there is nothing in the poem itself to justify doing so. While the poem is both powerful and direct, it is at the same time curiously detached and almost anonymous. Hardy achieves these qualities through two devices, both characteristic of his poems at their best. First, he makes the occasion particular in various ways—through the title, through the particular moment "when the weather changed," through the demonstrative "*That* night"; but at the same time he leaves it unspecified as to actual human circumstances and relationships. Second, he effects (and this is a very Hardyesque device) a displacement of the appropriate emotions, either by attributing them directly to natural objects (as when the tree "declared to the gloom/Its sorrow") or by implying them through the symbolic actions of natural things (here principally the weather and the dead leaves). The speaker remains passive and mute throughout the poem; only the natural world moves and bears meaning.

---

* Quotations from Hardy's own works and from the two volumes of biography published by his wife have been identified in the text as above, using short titles (for full bibliographical details, see below, p. 183). Notes which could not be handled conveniently in this way have been placed at the back of the book, and the usual superior numerals inserted in the text.

Like many of Hardy's best poems, "A Night in November" is built around a single symbolic action, an action *outside* the speaker, which touches him as the leaf touches his hand—accidentally and momentarily, and a little mysteriously. Hardy's sensitivity to such natural symbolic actions provided him with a powerful poetic instrument; but it also gave him a defense against personal confession and self-revelation. So long as he could realize the emotions in the fall of a leaf, he did not have to say: "I grieve."

When critics who admire Hardy speak of the man, they praise his "truth and goodness" or his "homely, tender, honest, and magnanimous" character.[5] These are admirable qualities, but they are somewhat remote—the qualities of a man we may admire, but can't know very well; they sum up the virtues of the personality that Hardy projected through his poems. We may regard this formal, withdrawn, courteously ironic pose as a "mask," in Yeats's sense of the term; certainly it operated as Yeats's mask did, providing Hardy with a detached position from which to say what he had to say. The mask was, I think, partly a defense against the Victorian public; Hardy was aware that his ideas were not popular ones, and he may have acted from a desire to remove personality from whatever controversy might arise. But it was also partly an expression of his own nature, and of the nature of his time, for Hardy was, in his sense of propriety and decorum, very much of his time, very much the proper Victorian.[6] Charles Morgan recognized this aspect of Hardy when, in his account of Hardy's 1920 visit to Oxford (where Morgan was then an undergraduate), he remarked that "he was not simple; he had the formal subtlety peculiar to his own generation; there was something deliberately 'ordinary' in his demeanour which was a concealment of extraordinary fires—a method of self-protection common enough in my grandfather's generation, though rare now" (*Later Years,* p. 209). Where revelation and reticence conflict, the mask is at least one answer; perhaps the only other answer is silence.

But, unlike Yeats, Hardy never let the mask slip, except perhaps in the 1912-13 elegies; one has no sense of the *other* man behind it. In everything he wrote, and in what portions of his private life we are permitted to glimpse, he was the speaking voice of his poems. The published accounts of visits with Hardy at Max Gate offer much the same picture: a gentle, remote old man, patting a dog. The most perceptive visitors (like Virginia Woolf) saw irony in the role. But there were not many such.

A mask may, as Yeats testified, free the poetic mind from the restrictions of its own inbrooding; but it will also impose its own restrictions—a mask is less pliable than the human face. Hardy's mask allowed him to write, but it restricted him to the poetry of ironic pessimism, and to reticence as a mode of expression.

All these qualifications and negative judgments which one may make of Hardy would seem to make him an "in spite of" poet—one of those whom the critic must first forgive in order to appreciate. But critics are not a forgiving lot, and in view of so many obvious flaws in the poetry it is easy to imagine a body of criticism entirely devoted to abuse. Hardy himself fostered the impression that this was true; he was morbidly sensitive to critical attack (though incapable of compromising himself to avoid it), and his notebooks and prefaces contain many bitter references to the hostility and stupidity of the "licensed tasters." There is scarcely any mention of approving, or even understanding criticism.

It is true that some of the early reviews of the poetry were unsympathetic, or simply stupid. Hardy had, in his last novels, done considerable violence to the cultivated taste of his time, and it is not surprising that *Wessex Poems,* coming only three years after *Jude,* should have been received with some hostility (though the reviews were not on the whole extreme). But by 1906, when the second volume of *The Dynasts* appeared, the press had shifted to Hardy's side, and subsequent volumes were, in general, as well received as they had any right to be. Charles Morgan, meeting Hardy in 1920, was surprised at the bitterness with which Hardy spoke of his critics. "The origin of this bitterness," Morgan wrote, "was in the past where, I believe, there was indeed good reason for it, but it was directed now against contemporary critics of his own work, and I could not understand what general reason he had to complain of them. He used no names; he spoke with studied reserve, sadly rather than querulously; but he was persuaded . . . that critics approached his work with an ignorant prejudice against his 'pessimism' which they allowed to stand in the way of fair reading and fair judgment" (*Later Years,* p. 208). This was not, of course, strictly the case. By 1920 many prominent critics, including Lytton Strachey and Middleton Murry, had reviewed his verse with sympathy and (at least in the case of Strachey) with intelligence.

Hardy might well have complained, however, of his more ambitious critics, the ones who wrote books about him. Since Lionel Johnson's study of the novels was published in 1894 there have been many books written on Hardy, but they have been concentrated on the fiction, to the virtual exclusion of the poetry. H. C. Duffin, in the first edition of his *Thomas Hardy* (1916), took no notice of the poems at all, though Hardy had by then published five volumes of verse and the three parts of *The Dynasts*. In his second edition Duffin allowed an appendix on the poetry, in which he observed, however, that "from the point of view of literary value. . . it is probable that no one of the eight volumes of Hardy's poetry is worth a single chapter from one of his major novels."[7] W. R. Rutland seemed to second Duffin when he wrote in his own book on Hardy that "the poetry is in the nature of a commentary on the novels."[8] This view of the poems as by-products runs through Hardy criticism from the earliest reviews, where it is perhaps pardonable, to the latest studies, where it is certainly not.[9]

Yet though Hardy's full-length critics have in general slighted the poetry, his position among English poets seems to have been taken for granted for many years. One year after Duffin's book appeared, Quiller-Couch included five poems by Hardy in his *Oxford Book of Victorian Verse,* and anthologies published since then have recognized Hardy's right to considerable space (Louis Untermeyer's mid-century edition of *Modern British Poetry* includes thirty Hardy poems—only Housman has more). The *Collected Poems* has never been out of print in either America or England since it first appeared (in England in 1919, in America in 1925); it has gone through twelve printings in the American edition.

One is tempted to conclude that we have here simply a case of radical disagreement between the professional critics and cultivated taste. Critical standards have certainly changed in the years since Hardy published his last volume, and not in a direction likely to make him a *maître d'école*. Cultivated taste has perhaps changed less.

Yet the "New Critics," though they have not given Hardy much attention, have treated his poems with sympathy and understanding when they have dealt with them at all. We have in the case of Hardy's critics as a whole not so much hostility as a failure of enthusiasm—the critics have not been unjust, but they have not been great partisans.

While we may recognize this circumstance as possibly significant in our final understanding of Hardy as a poet, we must treat the apparent disagreement between critics and readers with caution. It is difficult to establish "cultivated taste" when it appears to differ from the judgments of the professional critics, and especially when the critics are less antagonistic than simply silent; and it is obviously dangerous to regard popularity as in itself meritorious. The qualities of Hardy's verse which have led to the failure of enthusiasm still exist, and some at least are poetic flaws which no recital of sales and anthology selections will turn into virtues. Popular recognition and critical indifference constitute two facets of the single fact with which we are concerned.

"It is only maturer patience," says Ezra Pound, that impatient man, "that can sweep aside a writer's honest error, and overlook unaccomplished clumsiness or outlandishness or old-fashionedness, for the sake of the solid center. Thus many clever people have overlooked Thomas Hardy's verses, even though the author of the *Mayor of Casterbridge* lurks behind them."[10] This book is, at least in intention, an exercise in "maturer patience." It is not the critic's job, of course, to "sweep aside" or "overlook" aspects of his subject's work; if we pretend that *Desperate Remedies* and "My Cicely" do not exist, we will have at the end of our investigations not Hardy, but another, less fallible man. We must look at the failures, if only to understand the successes. But Pound is right about the "solid center": that is, or should be, our goal—to discover what it is, central to Hardy's art, that makes it what it is.

2

Hardy and the Poets

HARDY WAS, as I have said, a reticent man, and this reticence helped to create a false impression of his career in poetry which is not yet dissipated. Although he began to write poetry in his teens, some ten years before he wrote his first novel, he delayed publication of a book of poems until his fifty-eighth year. "*Writing* verse," he wrote to Cockerell, "gives me much pleasure, but not publishing it. I never did care much about publication, as I proved by my keeping some of the verses forty years in MS."[11] This remark is slightly disingenuous; Hardy did try to publish his early poems, and with some success. "The Bride-Night Fire" first appeared in 1875, and he apparently planned to include "some original verses" in *The Poor Man and the Lady*. It is true, however, that, when his reputation as a novelist would have made it possible for him to publish his poems, he delayed. The delay was, I think, a symbolic gesture on Hardy's part—novel-writing was creation on another, inferior level, and only when he was free to abandon it did he offer himself to the world as what he had in fact been all the time—a poet.

When Hardy did publish his first volume of poems, in 1898, he appeared as a leading and controversial novelist who had retired into poetry. The reviewers, quite understandably, read the poems in the light of the novels, looked for the same quarrels, and generally found them. It is inevitable, I suppose, that a man who has made his reputation in one literary form will have difficulty in establishing an equivalent and separate reputation in another; I can think of no poet-novelist who has achieved equal recognition in both forms. Hardy's case was particularly difficult, in that the poems did not appear at the same time as the novels, and so become interwoven with them in readers' minds. Hence the view of the poems as marginalia to the novels.

Hardy was also hampered by the *kind* of reputation he had made as a novelist. His novels, or at least the later ones, had come as shocks to the literary world. He was "a sort of village atheist brooding and blaspheming over the village idiot";[12] he was a "philosopher" in a pejorative sense, a thinker of unpleasant, pessimistic, morbid thoughts. The poems were therefore examined for their philosophy, and the accusations made which plagued Hardy for the rest of his life.

The dominance of Hardy's reputation as a novelist is ironic, in view of his own attitudes toward his two vocations. He told Cockerell that he would never have written a line of prose if he could have earned his living at poetry, and what evidence we have of his inclinations supports this statement.

We have, first of all, the evidence of the notebooks. Hardy's critical comments, scattered throughout the two volumes collected by Mrs. Hardy, are about evenly divided between matters of fiction and matters of poetry, though the former concern virtually disappears, as one might expect, after 1898. The remarks on poetry are invariably theoretical and technical ("the mission of poetry is . . .," "the ultimate aim of the poet should be . . ."), the remarks of a dedicated poet. Concerning fiction, on the other hand, Hardy could make such a statement as this:

> The truth is that I am willing, and indeed anxious, to give up any points which may be desirable in a story when read as a whole, for the sake of others which shall please those who read it in numbers. Perhaps I may have higher aims some day, and be a great stickler for the proper artistic balance of the completed work, but for the present circumstances lead me to wish merely to be considered a good hand at a serial (*Early Life,* p. 131).

This was written at the beginning of Hardy's career, in 1876. Obviously the day did come when he had higher aims, though he never became a "great stickler," and all but the best of his novels have a Gothic asymmetry about them. Even *The Mayor of Casterbridge,* considered by many critics his best-proportioned novel, was composed quite frankly as "mere journeywork"; "Hardy fancied he had damaged [it] more recklessly as an artistic whole," Mrs. Hardy wrote, "in the interest of the newspaper in which it appeared serially, than perhaps any other of his novels, his aiming to get an incident into almost every week's part causing him in his own judgment to add events to the narrative somewhat too freely" (*Early Life,* p. 235).

There are other examples of the indignities which Hardy was willing to practice on his novels in the interests of serial publication and "the conventions of the libraries"—the changes in *Tess* are the most famous, but there are also many in *Jude* and in other novels. "Of his verses, on the other hand," Ford Madox Ford wrote, "he was fiercely jealous. No one could have persuaded him to alter a word either in the interests of fluidity of metre or of the delicacies. The shocked *Cornhill* would have published *A Sunday Morning Tragedy* if he would have omitted some verses and changed others, and would have published 'Who now remembers Almack's balls?' if he would have altered a word or two...."[13] It was because of Hardy's "jealousy" that Ford met him; for, according to Ford, the *English Review* was established, with Ford as editor, specifically to publish "A Sunday Morning Tragedy" when no other periodical would.

Perhaps the integrity of Hardy's private, poetic life was paid for by this willingness to compromise in his public, novel-writing life. He was willing to do anything that a successful novelist should do—keep a notebook ("apparently with the idea that if one followed the trade of fiction one must take notes, rather than from natural tendency," Mrs. Hardy observed, *Early Life,* p. vii), live in London society during the season, take the girls out of Angel's arms and put them in a wheelbarrow—but he kept his poetry inviolate. By keeping it to himself until he had achieved a position where the world could not touch him, he preserved its individuality and originality. This may not have been a conscious strategy; it was nonetheless effective.

The notebooks and the dated poems show that during his career as a writer of fiction, while he was writing roughly one three-volume novel a year, Hardy yet found time to experiment with verse forms. Mrs. Hardy noted that

Among his papers were quantities of notes on rhythm and metre: with outlines and experiments in innumerable original measures, some of which he adopted from time to time. These verse skeletons were mostly blank, and only designated by the usual marks for long and short syllables, accentuations, etc., but they were occasionally made up of "nonsense verses"—such as, he said, were written when he was a boy by students of Latin prosody with the aid of a "Gradus" (*Later Years,* pp. 79-80).

The notion of the empty poetic mold, waiting to be filled with words, may seem naïve, and Hardy has been criticized for his mechanical, formalistic methods. Mrs. Hardy's remarks seem to me too vague to use as the basis for serious criticism, but they do show Hardy's lively interest in the technical aspects of his chosen art. There is also a vague teaser in the fact that his "skeletons" showed syllabication, accentuations, "etc." One is reminded of Hopkins' elaborate metrical notations.

In another passage Mrs. Hardy goes cautiously into the question of metrical irregularity.

In the reception of this [*Wessex Poems*] and later volumes of Hardy's poems there was, he said, as regards form, the inevitable ascription to ignorance of what was really choice after full knowledge. That the author loved the art of concealing art was undiscerned. For instance, as to rhythm. Years earlier he had decided that too regular a beat was bad art. He had fortified himself in his opinion by thinking of the analogy of architecture, between which art and that of poetry he had discovered, to use his own words, that there existed a close and curious parallel, both arts, unlike some others, having to carry a rational content inside their artistic form. He knew that in architecture cunning irregularity is of enormous worth, and it is obvious that he carried on into his verse, perhaps in part unconsciously, the Gothic art-principle in which he had been trained—the principle of spontaneity, found in mouldings, tracery, and such like—resulting in the "unforeseen" (as it has been called) character of his metres and stanzas, that of stress rather than of syllable, poetic texture rather than poetic veneer; the latter kind of thing, under the name of "constructed ornament", being what he, in common with every Gothic student, had been taught to avoid as the plague. He shaped his poetry accordingly, introducing metrical pauses, and reversed beats; and found for his trouble that some particular line of a poem exemplifying this principle was greeted with a would-be jocular remark that such a line "did not make for immortality" (*Later Years,* pp. 78-79).

Qualities of mind can be seen here which Hardy had in common with certain of his contemporaries: the interest in irregularity, the turn toward stress scansion, the concern with "texture." Much of this note would apply equally well to Hopkins or Bridges, or Patmore, or Morris, or Yeats.

In spite of the copiousness of the notebooks, it is difficult to establish from them the exact origins of Hardy's poetic theory and methods. For, while he had a great deal to say about poetry, he rarely wrote about poets, and then only to recount some social encounter, or some book read; so that, while one can easily count the references to Hardy's contemporaries in the notebooks, the sums prove only that Browning was dining out a great deal in those days, and that Hardy was reading.

References in the notebooks to things read are frequent, but unsatisfactory. Hardy went about the business of becoming a literary man with almost comic seriousness, like a burlesque of Milton at Horton. In his late twenties he decided that "as in verse was concentrated the essence of all imaginative and emotional literature, to read verse and nothing else was the shortest way to the fountain-head of such, for one who had not a great deal of spare time" (*Early Life,* p. 64); and for two years he read no prose other than newspapers and weekly reviews. The early notebooks are full of entries like these: "Read some Horace; also *Childe Harold* and *Lalla Rookh* till ½ past 12"; and (in 1875) "Read again Addison, Macaulay, Newman, Sterne, Defoe, Lamb, Gibbon, Burke, Times Leaders, etc., in a study of style." And even in 1887, a successful, mature author, he could proudly note: "Books read or pieces looked at this year," a list of twenty-seven authors and titles, from Aristophanes to "Ode to Grecian Urn" (*Early Life,* pp. 64, 138, 267). Hardy rarely expressed his own judgment of these self-improving texts, and it is difficult to determine the effects of, say, the *Times* leaders on his style.

There is little indication that Hardy read much of the work of his better-known contemporaries, either poets or novelists, or that he admired any of them greatly. Late in life he recalled that "I used to walk from my lodgings near Hyde Park to the draughting office every morning, never without a copy of the first edition of the *Poems and Ballads* [of Swinburne] sticking out of my pocket." This sounds like a confession of influence, but in the next sentence he added, with what seems conscious irony, "It was a borrowed copy . . . if I'd only bought it at the time, it would be worth many guineas today."[14] The influence, if any, was ideological rather than poetical; Hardy's letters to and about Swinburne make much of the latter's role in the world (Hardy regarded him as a martyr to freedom of thought), but say little about the poetry; and his memorial poem, "A Singer Asleep," is a weak, conventional elegy.

Of the other poets Hardy knew, Patmore sent him a volume of verse, but there is no evidence that the gift was either read or acknowledged. Hardy did know his Browning; he specifically mentions "The Statue and the Bust" as "one of the finest of Browning's poems," and he shows that he had read *The Ring and the Book* and "A Grammarian's Funeral." The poem on Meredith suggests that Hardy had read *Modern Love,* and admired the theme (one would expect him to). And there are two passing references to Tennyson in the *Collected Poems*. Virtually no other direct reference to contemporary poetry (other than a few brief quotations scattered through the novels) occurs in either the notebooks, the novels, or the poems.[15]

There is even less to indicate that Hardy felt any debt to his fellow novelists, or indeed to any novelist. He met most of his famous contemporaries socially—James, Meredith, Kipling, Stevenson, Bret Harte, Howells, Conrad, Wells, Gorky, Bennett, and Forster are mentioned by Mrs. Hardy, generally as dinner companions—but there is almost no criticism of other writers' fiction in the notebooks.[16] In the case of poet-novelists like Scott and Meredith, Hardy preferred the poetry. He "never ceased to regret that the author of 'the most Homeric poem in the English language—*Marmion*'—should later have declined on prose fiction" (*Early Life,* p. 64); and he observed with some puzzlement that, though Meredith's novels had "some poetry" and James's "no grain" of it, "yet I can read James when I cannot look at Meredith" (*Later Years,* p. 169).

It is particularly striking, therefore, that Hardy did acknowledge one direct debt, and that to a poet—his Dorset friend, William Barnes. Hardy's references to Barnes are frequent and reverent, in sharp contrast to his reticence toward other contemporaries; he frankly acknowledged the older man as his master, and an intimate influence on his work. "I have lived too much within his atmosphere," he wrote to Patmore in 1886, "to see his productions in their due perspective, as you see them."[17] The friendship, which began in 1856 when Hardy worked next door to Barnes's school, remained close until the latter's death thirty years later. Hardy reviewed Barnes's *Poems of Life in the Dorset Dialect;* he wrote his friend's obituary notice for the

Athenaeum; he edited and wrote a preface for Barnes's *Selected Poems;* and he wrote one of his finest elegies, "The Last Signal," on the occasion of Barnes's death. Nowhere does he show such close emotional bonds to another person, except in the sequence of elegies to his first wife, the "Poems of 1912-13."

The similarities between the two poets seem so obvious that it is tempting to explain the attraction which Hardy felt toward Barnes's work as simply a case of like attracting like. After all, they were both Dorset poets, both rustic in origin, both provincial in literary taste, both interested in humble folk and the dialect they spoke. What could be more natural than that they should work together?

If one examines the two more closely, however, these surface similarities disappear. In the first place, Barnes and Hardy are not "Dorset poets" in the same sense. Barnes was a provincial, Hardy was not. That is, Barnes drew upon those qualities of his region which were unique—the speech, the customs, the local types—for his characteristic poetic qualities. When Hardy drew upon Dorset in his poems it was not for such local color, but for universally valid symbols, derived from weather, seasons, and human and natural hardships. "Provincial" in this sense is not necessarily pejorative, but it does indicate a certain narrowness of vision in Barnes which Hardy does not share. The fact that Hardy was not content to use Dorset as a place name is significant; his Wessex, like Faulkner's Yoknapatawpha, is a self-made reality, precise in definition, but ruled only by the laws of the artist's imagination.

As for dialect, there is little of it in Hardy's poems—little, that is, of the literal sort that Barnes affected. Hardy said of Barnes, "He never tampered with the dialect itself"

(Preface to *Barnes,* p. ix). Hardy, on the other hand, tampered with it a good deal, made it do his bidding, introducing dialectal vocabulary when it suited his poetic aims and omitting it when it didn't. In the 1898 preface to *Wessex Poems* Hardy wrote:

Whenever an ancient and legitimate word of the district, for which there was no equivalent in received English, suggested itself as the most natural, nearest, and often only expression of a thought, it has been made use of, on what seemed good grounds (*Collected Poems,* p. iii).

The grounds were aesthetic, and not, as often seems the case with Barnes, philological.

The only poems in Hardy's *Collected Poems* which are dialectal in Barnes's manner are the early "The Bride-Night Fire" (1866) and "Valenciennes," a ballad recited by Corp'l Tullidge in *The Trumpet Major,* and suited to his rustic delivery. Elsewhere, the use of dialect is largely confined to isolated words, with occasional idiomatic phrases and elisions. Phonetic spelling, which makes Barnes's dialect poems a wilderness of *v*'s and *z*'s and umlauts, appears in Hardy only in an occasional voiced sibilant, as in "Zunday" for "Sunday" in "The Curate's Kindness." It is as false to call Hardy a dialect poet as it would be to call Barnes anything else.

If the supposed similarity between the two poets is weak, the dissimilarities are strong enough. There is, primarily, the point of view; it is difficult to imagine two men more antithetical in their attitudes toward existence. Hardy's was what Meredith called a "twilight view of life"; Barnes saw "a harmony of the whole with the good of man." Darwin stands between them, giving Hardy's poems a somber cast which Barnes's do not have. Furthermore, the "narrowness of vision" which I ascribed to Barnes extends to his choice of theme and treatment; he is rarely speculative or meditative as Hardy is, seldom touches on the large poetic themes. His field is rustic anecdote, and he cultivates it well, within its boundaries.

Hardy was clearly aware of these basic dissimilarities. In his obituary notice on Barnes he wrote:

> Mr. Barnes never assumed the high conventional style; and he entirely leaves alone ambition, pride, despair, defiance, and other of the grander passions which move mankind great and small. His rustics are, as a rule, happy people, and very seldom feel the sting of the rest of modern mankind—the disproportion between the desire for serenity and the power of obtaining it. . . . Their pathos, after all, is the attribute upon which the poems must depend for their endurance; and the incidents which embody it are those of everyday cottage life, tinged throughout with that 'light that never was,' which the emotional art of the lyrist can project upon the commonest things (*Life and Art,* pp. 53-54).

The obverse of this poetic character is obviously a self-portrait of Hardy himself.

Yet, for all their dissimilarities, Hardy admired Barnes as a poet and sought him as a master. He visited the older poet whenever he could, and his copies of Barnes's poems show heavy and careful annotation. One would expect that such a relationship would be "influential"; the question is, how? What was there in Barnes's poems that Hardy could use?

There was, primarily, a dramatic form, a form particularly suited to Hardy's abilities and needs. In his preface to Barnes's *Selected Poems,* Hardy described its value:

> Even if he [Barnes] often used the dramatic form of peasant speakers as a pretext for the expression of his own mind and ex-

periences—which cannot be doubted—yet he did not always do this, and the assumed character of husbandman or hamleteer enabled him to elude in his verse those dreams and speculations that cannot leave alone the mystery of things,—possibly an unworthy mystery and disappointing if solved, though one that has a harrowing fascination for many poets,—and helped him to fall back on dramatic truth, by making his personages express the notions of life prevalent in their sphere (pp. xi-xii).

This conception of the poem-as-drama is, I think, the one thing for which Hardy is directly indebted to Barnes, as the quotation above seems to suggest. There is also an obvious debt to Browning's dramatic monologues, and there were other Victorian poets writing in this same general vein, but Hardy differs from most of them in that his monologues are less concerned with the creation of character than with the presentation of a view of the world, a "dramatic truth" for which the speaker is a more or less anonymous voice (something much the same might be said of Hardy's novels).

In preface after preface Hardy asserted the dramatic character of his poems, "and this even where they are not obviously so." He insisted that even "those lyrics penned in the first person ... are to be regarded, in the main, as dramatic monologues by different characters" (*Collected Poems,* pp. iii and 175). Many poems carry stage directions, and are cast in dialogue (as are some of Barnes's). Even his most philosophical poems are likely to be set in dramatic form, in unlikely, sometimes floundering conversations involving men, creatures, and purblind Doomsters.

The merit of individual poems is sometimes slight, but the merit of the method is considerable. It satisfied Hardy's compulsive reticence, and it freed him from poetic subjectivity; by creating a new speaking voice for the poem he removed himself from the stage (though he can generally be discerned in the wings, cranking the machinery). Further, the method enabled him to be a speculative poet without being a ruminator, to avoid "those dreams and speculations that cannot leave alone the mystery of things" by the device of giving dramatic identities to his abstract ideas.

Hardy once observed of Barnes that, while "primarily spontaneous, he was academic closely after" (Preface to *Barnes*, p. ix). In this role of scholar of poetry Barnes exercised a highly beneficial influence on Hardy, for he introduced his young disciple to forms outside the main stream of English poetry which Hardy, with his limited education, would probably not have discovered for himself. The late nineteenth century, like the Renaissance, revitalized English poetry with grafts from other traditions. The role of Barnes in this process has never been adequately evaluated. It seems to me considerable.

Barnes was a man of wide and curious learning. He wrote his diary in Italian, read some Persian every week, and drew upon sixty languages in the compilation of his *Philological Grammar*. He studied Welsh poetry, and employed Welsh metrical devices long before Hopkins did (of Barnes's Welsh experiments, Hopkins wrote to Patmore, "To tell the truth, I think I could do that better";[18] he was quite right, but Barnes did it first). Welsh, Persian and Italian verse forms appear in Barnes's poems, and Hardy borrowed a number of them—"The Mother Mourns," for example, is in a Persian stanza, the *ghazal,* which Barnes used in "The Knoll." (Tennyson also used it in the song "Now sleeps the crimson petal" in *The Princess,* and Hardy may have found it there, but Barnes seems a more likely source.) Hardy's memorial poem to Barnes, "The Last Signal," employs Welsh techniques introduced into English poetry by Barnes. Here is the first stanza:

> Silently I footed by an uphill road
> That led from my abode to a spot yew-boughed;
> Yellowly the sun sloped low down to westward,
> And dark was the east with cloud.
>
> (Collected Poems, p. 444)

The internal rhyme scheme ("road-abode") is called in Welsh poetry *union;* Barnes used it in "Times o' Year." There is also in Hardy's poem the repetitive consonantal pattern called in Welsh *cynghanedd;* in the third line, for example, the pattern is LLSNSLLNS (compare Barnes's use of the device in "My orcha'd in Linden Lea"). Hardy's further use of assonance, or vowel chime, makes this one of his finest poems from a purely technical point of view. The poem also seems to me a clear demonstration of a case in which a direct influence may be legitimately inferred.

It is significant that admiration of Barnes was not limited to Hardy among late Victorian poets. Hopkins called him "a perfect artist," and set two of his poems to music; Patmore titled his article on Barnes "An English Classic." These poets admired in Barnes those things which were characteristic of their own poetry—precision of observation, an expansion of the poetic vocabulary, and technical control: ". . . he is always classic both in form and substance," Patmore wrote,[19] and Hardy added, "We find him warbling his native wood-notes with a watchful eye on the predetermined score" (Preface to *Barnes,* p. ix).

Barnes's view of the world was microcosmic—narrow but detailed. "Look for pleasure," he wrote,

> at the line of beauty, and other curves of charming grace in the wind-blown stems of grass, and bowing barley or wheat: in the water-shaken bulrush, in the leaves of plants, and in the petals of flowers; in the outlines of birds, and even their feathers and eggs; in the flowing lines of the greyhound, the horse and cat, and other animals; in the shell of the mollusc, and in the wings and markings of insects; in the swell of the downy cheek, the rounded chin, the flowing bending of the pole and back, and the outswelling and inwinding lines from the head to the leg of woman stepping onward in the pride of youthful grace; and tell us whether nature does not show us graceful curves enough to win us from ugliness, even in a porringer.[20]

Examples of this kind of observation in Barnes's poems are innumerable—one might say it *is* the poetry. The same sensitive precision of description is one of Hardy's great merits. His "Afterwards" might almost be a versification of the prose passage from Barnes quoted above; and there are many similar "nature" poems in the works of Hardy's contemporaries, in Hopkins, Bridges, and Meredith. When Hopkins, in a letter to Bridges, praised Barnes's poems for "their Westcountry 'instress,'" he was saying, in his own odd way, that Barnes had been most successful in capturing the essential nature of Dorset in his poems. In a later letter to Patmore, he went on:

> He comes, like Homer and all poets of native epic, provided with epithets, images, and so on which seem to have been tested and digested for a long age in their native air and circumstances and to have a *keeping* which nothing else could give; but in fact they are rather all of his own finding and first throwing off. This seems to me very high praise.[21]

Hardy, in his writings on Barnes, was anxious to assert the existence in Barnes's poetry of a quality which he shared with his master, which he called "closeness of phrase to his vision."

His ingenious internal rhymes, his subtle juxtapositions of kindred lippings and vowel-sounds, show a fastidiousness in word-selection that is surprising in verse which professes to represent the habitual modes of language among the western peasantry. We do not find in the dialect balladists of the seventeenth century, or in Burns (with whom he has sometimes been measured), such careful finish, such verbal dexterities, such searchings for the most cunning syllables, such satisfaction with the best phrase (Preface to *Barnes*, pp. ix-x).

One might compare this verbal dexterity with Hopkins' Anglo-Saxon and Welsh coinings, and with Bridges' experiments, as well as with Hardy's own expanded vocabulary. Barnes's movement away from conventional, circumscribed poetic diction, toward greater freedom and accuracy and "careful finish" anticipated a more general development in the same direction in the generation of poets that followed him.

We can, I think, make two valid statements about Barnes's influence on Hardy: he is the only poet, with the obvious exception of Shakespeare, whose influence is demonstrable; and the direction of his influence is the direction taken by English poetry in the transitional period between High Victorianism and the twentieth century. It is important, in considering Hardy as a poet, to remember that he had masters other than Darwin and Huxley, and that he acknowledged poetic, as well as philosophical debts. It is perhaps even more important to recognize the fact that he shared certain of those debts with his contemporaries, and that he was, in many ways, at one with the "advanced" poets of his time. We can use their common admiration for Barnes's poetry as a device for pointing the link which ties Hardy to Hopkins and Patmore, two poets with whom one would not ordinarily associate him. The differences among these three are, of course, considerable. But there are marked similarities as well—primarily in their common experimentalism in metrics and diction, and in their intensely personal, eccentric modes of expression. All three poets were poetic revolutionists of a sort, rebelling against what they regarded as an exhausted tradition, and seeking a new idiom for poetry. Such a statement need scarcely be made of Hopkins now—his role in the making of the modern poetic idiom is a critical commonplace—but it is worth making about Hardy, whose originality is less emphasized, perhaps because it is less flamboyant.

This is not to argue, of course, that Barnes exercised an equally direct influence on the development of these three poets; nevertheless, their common admiration for him is revealing, because it suggests that they shared certain ideas about poetry and had certain common values. Barnes offered them an example of qualities in poetry which they recognized as desirable; when they came to express those qualities in their own poetry, they pursued their own idiosyncratic ways and created their own, highly personal styles.

But while Hopkins' style has been a principal concern for his critics, the same has not been true of Hardy. There are, I think, two reasons for this difference: first, there is the technique itself; the oddness of Hopkins' verse is immediately apparent and must be dealt with at once in order to get into the poems at all; Hardy's originality is less striking and therefore less pressing—one can read his poems without worrying about the style. Second, there is belief: Hopkins, the Jesuit priest, offers no serious problems; that is to say, believing *is* the problem of his poems, but there is no question of the *object* of belief—we do not have to define Hopkins' God. Hardy, on the other hand, is heterodox and queer, full of strange personifications and inscrutable forces; we must figure out what God and Nature and Crass Casualty are about before we can go on to an understanding of the poems. Hence Hopkins the devotional poet is read more for the poetry than for the devotion, while Hardy the philosophical poet is read more for the philosophy than for the poetry. Our concern here is ultimately with the poetry, but before we can go further in considering it, we must look at the ways in which it is possible to regard Hardy as a philosophical poet.

3

The Uses of Philosophy

ONE POINT ABOUT Hardy upon which critics seem to agree is that he had a philosophy. They may say, as T. S. Eliot does, that "Hardy's work would be better for a better philosophy, or none at all";[22] nevertheless, the common view is that the philosophy must be dealt with because, as Eliot adds, "there it is." This is curious if one considers that it *isn't* there in the sense that it is in the work of a number of other modern poets. Hardy did not try to organize his beliefs into a prose treatise, as Yeats did in *A Vision;* he did not write elaborate notes to his poems explaining the fine philosophical points, as Auden did in *New Year Letter;* he did not attempt anything as ex cathedra as *After Strange Gods* or *Notes Toward a Definition of Culture.* Yet, for Hardy's critics, there it is, and there it continues to be.

If we look for reasons for this curious critical interest in Hardy the thinker, we will find, I think, two. First, Hardy did write a number of poems which are overtly, aggressively "philosophical," poems like "A Philosophical Fantasy," to which he attached as an epigraph Bagehot's remark that "Milton . . . made God argue." The epigraph is appropriate to the occasion, and to many other occasions as well, for Hardy's God, when he speaks, is as argumentative as Milton's, and for the same reason: Hardy was also attempting, in his own ironic way, to justify God's ways to man. Hence the poems in which God argues, Nature complains, and Man questions. The obviousness of the ideas in these poems has made them fair game for the philosophical critic, and the result has been an imbalance of criticism in the direction of poems which are neither Hardy's best nor his most characteristic.

For the second reason, Hardy is entirely responsible: he insisted that he be dealt with as a "thinker." He was self-conscious about the philosophical content of his poems and morbidly sensitive to the public's response to it. His occasional statements in self-defense were most often rebuttals to philosophical criticisms, and when he set about to argue his case at length in the "Apology" to *Late Lyrics and Earlier,* he spoke as a thinker in defense of his ideas and not as a poet. Yet at the same time that he defended his thinking, Hardy was anxious to deny that it was systematic. In the same "Apology" he described his view of life as "really a series of fugitive impressions which I have never tried to co-ordinate"; and this statement is paraphrased in other prefaces and in his letters.

Hardy's most elaborate defense of his philosophical verse is contained in a letter to Alfred Noyes, written in response to a public lecture by the latter criticizing Hardy's "pessimistic" philosophy. In the letter Hardy reasserts his position as a disclaimer of systematic intentions, but he adds:

Also . . . I should have to remind him ["a man of letters," i.e., Noyes] of the vast difference between the expression of fancy and the expression of belief. My imagination may have often run away with me; but all the same, my sober opinion—so far as I have any definite one—of the Cause of Things, has been defined in scores of places, and is that of a great many ordinary thinkers: that the said Cause is neither moral nor immoral, but *un*moral: 'loveless and hateless' I have called it, 'which neither good nor evil knows' . . . This view is quite in keeping with what you call a Pessimistic philosophy (a mere nickname with no sense in it), which I am quite unable to see as 'leading logically to the conclusion that the Power behind the universe is malign' (*Later Years*, pp. 216-17).

The revealing point here is the distinction between the "expression of fancy" and the "expression of belief," a distinction which Hardy makes, rather oddly, in terms of the way in which he addresses "the Power behind the universe." "In my fancies, or poems of the imagination," Hardy explains,

I have of course called this Power all sorts of names—never supposing they would be taken for more than fancies. I have even in prefaces warned readers to take them as such—as mere impressions of the moment, exclamations in fact. But it has always been my misfortune to presuppose a too intelligent reading public, and no doubt people will go on thinking that I really believe the Prime Mover to be a malignant old gentleman, a sort of King of Dahomey—an idea which, so far from my holding it, is to me irresistibly comic (*Later Years*, p. 217).

This seems to say, or at least to imply, that the "expressions of fancy" are the poems which dress their philosophy in metaphor—poems, that is, like "Nature's Questioning," "New Year's Eve," and "God's Education." The other category, poems which are "expressions of belief," includes, as Hardy explains in the same letter, certain "definitions in *The Dynasts* as well as in short poems." He does not specify here *which* short poems, but in another letter he remarks that the first and second parts of *The Dynasts* and some of the poems in *Poems of the Past and the Present* "exhibit fairly enough the whole philosophy" (*Later Years*, p. 125); and I think we may take as "expressions of belief" poems like "The Mother Mourns," "To Life," "The Problem," and "'ΑΓΝΩΣΤΩι ΘΕΩι."

Hardy is saying, then, that a poet is not philosophically responsible for those ideas which he expresses in metaphor, but only for his "definitions," his direct statements. Such an assertion reveals an essential contradiction in Hardy's mind; he saw art as a criticism of life, yet he seemed unwilling to accept responsibility for the poetic use he made of his own ideas. It is perhaps too glib to say simply that the poet and the philosopher in Hardy were in conflict; yet the two attitudes toward experience—as "fugitive impressions" to be recorded and as life to be criticized—which Hardy expresses do correspond to conflicting concerns, and they help to explain the confusion in his mind which he was never able to resolve. Being a conscientious man, Hardy desired to be philosophically consistent; but he was aware that "fancy" might lead him in directions which philosophy could not justify. The explanation to Noyes explains nothing: it merely confesses the conflict.

Actually, comparatively few of Hardy's poems—perhaps 5 per cent—could be called strictly philosophical (I would define a philosophical poem as one in which concepts function as the content rather than as the intellectual substructure). These include primarily Hardy's argumentative poems—poems like "The Mother Mourns," "Doom and She," "The Subalterns," and "God-Forgotten." Some of these Hardy would probably wish to call "expressions of fancy," but all are more or less overt in their philosophizing, and none is an entirely successful poem.

Hardy gives us an idea of how these poems were composed in a notebook entry dated 1883: "Poem. We [human beings] have reached a degree of intelligence which Nature never contemplated when framing her laws, and for which she consequently has provided no adequate satisfactions" (*Early Life,* p. 213). This is one of Hardy's persistent notions—we find it in a number of his philosophical poems, and in the novels as well—but the point here is that he starts with the idea, the abstract formulation, and sets off from it in the direction of poetry. We are inclined, and I think rightly, to mistrust the method.

Hardy's sonnet, "The Sleep-Worker," is a case in point—an idea very like that quoted above, versified as an "expression of belief."

> When wilt thou wake, O Mother, wake and see—
> As one who, held in trance, has laboured long
> By vacant rote and prepossession strong—
> The coils that thou hast wrought unwittingly;
>
> Wherein have place, unrealized by thee,
> Fair growths, foul cankers, right enmeshed with wrong,
> Strange orchestras of victim-shriek and song,
> And curious blends of ache and ecstasy?—
>
> Should that morn come, and show thy opened eyes
> All that Life's palpitating tissues feel,
> How wilt thou bear thyself in thy surprise?—
>
> Wilt thou destroy, in one wild shock of shame,
> Thy whole high heaving firmamental frame,
> Or patiently adjust, amend, and heal?
>
> (*Collected Poems,* pp. 110-11)

This is a bad poem, and we can describe its badness readily without reference to the belief which it expresses; we can say simply that the poet has failed to control his metaphorical structure. On the one hand, running through the poem is the anthropomorphic metaphor of nature as a mother asleep. Although asserted in the first line, this metaphor is not developed; the title of the poem substitutes a rather different impression, and nature in the poem demonstrates no maternal qualities (the title seems to prevent our taking "labour" in the second line as anything more motherly than work). The relation of the mother to the force which holds her "in trance," a very basic question, one would think, is entirely ignored.

Superimposed upon this basic metaphor is a sequence of images, unrelated to the Mother or to each other, except as they independently illustrate stages in the "argument." There is no discernible development, for example, from *trance* through *strange orchestras* to *morn* and *palpitating tissues;* the relationship is simply that all the images can be applied separately to aspects of Hardy's convictions about nature.

If this is true, then we must conclude that while the failure of the poem can be *described* entirely in terms of its metaphors it can be *explained* only with reference to Hardy's philosophical preoccupations. Hardy subordinated the unity of his poem to the development of his idea; he violated the integrity of his materials to make his philosophical point. In the conflict between fancy and belief, to use the terms of Hardy's own distinction, belief won.

In making this distinction Hardy confessed to a basic tension in his mind and art, but he also pointed to a problem which is central to modern (that is, post-Darwinian) poetry. The problem of belief is one which any critic of poetry of the last hundred years must face. English poets from Matthew Arnold to Dylan Thomas have been confronted with essentially the same issue: how to make poetry out of experience which has no invested meaning. Yeats defined the problem in his *Autobiographies* when he described how Huxley and Tyndall deprived him of "the simple-mind religion of my childhood"[23] and how he tried to make a new religion of poetry; the problem for Hardy was the same, though the solution was different. Eventually Yeats found a new dualism; Hardy tried to make a poetry of monistic materialism. Yeats, because he was Irish and perhaps because he came later in the process, managed to find a new way of imposing symbolic significance upon matter and events; Hardy didn't. This is ironic if we consider that it was Hardy who attempted intellectual respectability, Yeats who went in for fairies and gyres and the ghosts of roses. *A Vision* is a farrago of spiritualism, mysticism, and the occult; Hardy, on the other hand, was in the main line of Victorian rationalism, and it was this rationalism that maimed his imagination and divided his mind. It convinced him that knowledge was available to reason and logic, and that truth was that which is verifiable; it excluded the spiritual, the intuitive, the mystical; and it led him toward systematic thought for which he was unqualified either by natural bent or by training. And in the end it failed him. He needed a metaphysic and he got Herbert Spencer.[24]

For the reader of Hardy's poetry, it is the failure and not the philosophy that is important, for it provides a key to Hardy's basic poetic nature. Hardy the poet found rationalism inadequate to his artistic needs; imagination, as he told Noyes, does run away with him, and for this we can be thankful. Hampered by a philosophy which he only partly understood and could only partly assimilate, he took, no doubt unconsciously, the poetic course—he reduced philosophy (at least in his best poems) to the folk level of belief, to superstition, to a sense of the impenetrable, contradictory mysteries of existence.

In a later letter to Noyes, Hardy wrote, "Yes, the whole scheme is incomprehensible, and there I suppose we must leave it—perhaps for the best. Knowledge might be terrible."[25] He is confessing his philosophical failure, but he is also inadvertently suggesting the nature of his poetic greatness. For it is this superstitious sense of terrible knowledge, of the irrational violence in the world which reason could not explain away, that gives Hardy's poetry its peculiar power. As a thinker he wrestled with the disparities and inequities of existence all his life, without ever finding an adequate solution; like Virginia Woolf's Mr. Ramsay, he could not get from Q to R. His poetry is about the effort, and the failures, not about the answers. It is philosophical insofar as the problems with which he was obsessed might also concern a philosopher, but it does not contain a philosophy.

Nevertheless, Hardy's struggles with the meaning of things, while they do not emerge in a system, do provide a method of approaching the poetry; for the sense of contradictions which he could not resolve is at the core of everything he wrote. One might say that his philosophical failure provided him with a way of seeing which, paradoxically, gave order to his art, though not ultimately to his world. That way of seeing we customarily call irony, meaning by that term a view of life which recognizes that experience is open to multiple interpretations, of which no *one* is simply right, and that the co-existence of incongruities is a part of the structure of existence. Now to assert that Hardy's poetry is ironic in tone is certainly to say nothing new; but I would argue that the fundamental function of irony in Hardy's work is not as tone or texture (though irony is certainly present in these terms, as we shall see when we examine Hardy's diction and imagery), but as a principle of structure, and that this is true both of the novels and of the poems. If this assertion is valid, then in turning from Hardy the philosopher to Hardy the ironist, we turn from an essentially irrelevant to a profoundly relevant aspect of his art.

The irony in Hardy's novels is readily apparent, and most of the commentators have dealt with it at length. I will content myself with one minor example from *Tess*, a sentence concerning the milkmaids who love Angel Clare so hopelessly: "They tossed and turned on their little beds, and the cheese-wring dripped monotonously downstairs" (p. 188). Love and cheese-wrings: Hardy saw the world as made up of such juxtapositions, each term ironically qualifying the other, but never fused into a single, comprehensive meaning. He is at his best when he is content simply to realize such ironic incongruities; he is at his worst when he moves from the felt irony of existence to explanation, at which point the Immanent Will, the President of the Immortals, and such personae take over.

The ironic structure of the novels should be as clear as the ironic texture, but it has not always been so to Hardy's critics. The famous coincidences, for example, have usually been criticized as ineptitudes of plotting; they are, rather, the structural equivalent of love and cheese-wrings. Things happen in improbable, and usually disastrous, sequences in Hardy's novels because life itself is an ironic form. "In the ill-judged execution of the well-judged plan of things," Hardy says in *Tess,* "the call seldom produces the comer, the man to love rarely coincides with the hour for loving" (pp. 48-49). And more succinctly in *Jude*: "But nobody did come, because nobody does" (p. 32).

The ambiguous situations which Hardy's ironic habits of mind led him to create have troubled some critics: Albert Guerard complains, for example, of the final episode in *A Pair of Blue Eyes* that "Hardy finds it hard to decide whether Elfride's funeral train . . . should be considered more ludicrous than tragic or more tragic than ludicrous."[26] But the point is that Hardy found it impossible to decide; the episode was at once ludicrous and tragic, and choice between the two attitudes was an entirely subjective one, for which the universe provided no rules. "If you look beneath the surface of any farce," he wrote, "you see a tragedy; and, on the contrary, if you blind yourself to the deeper issues of a tragedy you see a farce" (*Early Life,* p. 282). Tragedy and farce, that is, are relative, simply alternate ways of seeing an event; they are not attributes of the event itself. The farce beneath the tragic surface may be a cosmic farce, the sport of the President of the Immortals, but it is always there.

Hardy provided a handy illustration of this point in the first version of his poem "A Wife in London" when he subtitled the two sections "The Tragedy," in which the wife receives a telegram reporting the death of her husband in battle, and "The Irony," in which on the next day the postman brings a letter

> Fresh—firm—penned in highest feather—
> Page-full of his hoped return,
> And of home-planned jaunts by brake and burn
> In the summer weather,
> And of new love that they would learn.

(Collected Poems, pp. 83-84)

He dropped the subtitles from the version of the poem included in *Collected Poems*—persuaded, apparently, that the irony was self-evident—but the point of the poem remains the same. Tragedy and irony are set together, but as the universe provided Hardy no clue, the poem provides us none by which to choose between them; we have the experience, but not the meaning.

The two-part division of "A Wife in London" provides a simple example of the way in which Hardy's ironic view determined the structure of his work. He saw experience as a configuration of opposites, every event contradicted or qualified by a succeeding event, an infinite sequence of destructive tensions. Of the critical terms available to describe such a configuration, I suggest we adopt Yeats's *antinomial* rather than *dialectical,* for two reasons: first, because, although thesis and antithesis are always present in Hardy's structural patterns, there is rarely anything that could be described as a synthesis; and second, because the term points in passing to an interesting resemblance between Yeats and Hardy in their characteristic structural strategy.

Briefly, Hardy's antinomial pattern works this way: thesis (usually a circumstance commonly accepted as good—marriage, youth, young love, the reunion of husband and wife) is set against antithesis (infidelity, age, death, separation) to form an ironic complex, which is left unresolved. One might, generally speaking, say that the pattern is built on the relation of appearance and reality. In many of the poems this is true on a very simple level, as in "A Wife in London" or "Architectural Masks," which contrasts the exteriors of two houses with their occupants. But in more complicated poems the generalization is only valid if we recognize that appearance has its own kind of subjective truth—deluded love is still love—and is not merely an illusion to be destroyed; or to put it another way, reality is not morally superior to appearance, though it is always more powerful and always destructive.

It is in terms of this appearance-reality relationship that the inconsistencies of Hardy's philosophy are most apparent —in his poetry he could not be true to his pessimistic vision. Words like "lovingkindness" and "life-loyalties" creep in in spite of the philosophy, and the darkling thrush sings of "some blessed Hope, whereof he knew/And I was unaware." Perhaps no poet could be consistently ateleologically deterministic and remain a poet; for Hardy, at any rate, it is this antinomial tension between his thought and his feelings that gives his verse its characteristic pattern and its integrity, and which gives order, though a minimal order, to the chaos of experience.

The antinomial structure is most apparent in Hardy's most obviously ironic poems, like the "Satires of Circumstance" (Hardy used *satire* and *irony* interchangeably), but the better poems also have it, and draw from it a complexity which the weaker do not have. On the most obvious level, Hardy's antinomial set of mind is evident in his habit of dividing his poems into two parts: in the first part one term is set up, in the second its opposite is set against it, and their mutual antagonisms are ironically, but dispassionately remarked. Often Hardy made the pattern more obvious by using a two-stanza form, or two numbered sections, each devoted to one term of the antinomy, as in "A Merrymaking in Question," "Before and After Summer," "The Coquette and After"; the titles of the last two are further indications of the two-part structure, as well as of the role time plays in it.

This characteristic structure can be demonstrated in virtually any one of Hardy's nine-hundred-odd poems; I will take as a single example one of his commonest anthology pieces, "The Convergence of the Twain."

I
In a solitude of the sea
Deep from human vanity,
And the Pride of Life that planned her, stilly couches she.

II
Steel chambers, late the pyres
Of her salamandrine fires,
Cold currents thrid, and turn to rhythmic tidal lyres.

III
Over the mirrors meant
To glass the opulent
The sea-worm crawls—grotesque, slimed, dumb, indifferent.

IV
Jewels in joy designed
To ravish the sensuous mind
Lie lightless, all their sparkles bleared and black and blind.

V
Dim moon-eyed fishes near
Gaze at the gilded gear
And query: "What does this vaingloriousness down here?" . . .

VI
Well: while was fashioning
This creature of cleaving wing,
The Immanent Will that stirs and urges everything

VII

Prepared a sinister mate
For her—so gaily great—
A Shape of Ice, for the time far and dissociate.

VIII

And as the smart ship grew
In stature, grace, and hue,
In shadowy silent distance grew the Iceberg too.

IX

Alien they seemed to be:
No mortal eye could see
The intimate welding of their later history,

X

Or sign that they were bent
By paths coincident
On being anon twin halves of one august event,

XI

Till the Spinner of the Years
Said "Now!" And each one hears,
And consummation comes, and jars two hemispheres.

(*Collected Poems*, pp. 288-89)

Here the thesis is obviously the "smart ship," the antithesis the iceberg. The poem divides into two equal parts at stanza VI, the first part establishing the qualities of the thesis-term, the second introducing the antithesis. This is the most obvious antinomial pattern in the poem, but there are also a number of ancillary ones. The diction, for example, is of two distinct kinds: the lush, exotic, polysyllabic language of the first part works against the monosyllables of the second. The first part is heavy with modifiers, with active verbs, with particular, physical substantives; the second is bare and abstract by comparison.

Virtually all of the poem's imagery is concentrated in the description of the ship; the iceberg is simply a "Shape of Ice" growing "in shadowy silent distance."

The final stanza brings the two complex terms of the antinomy—by now they are ship-world and iceberg-world—together, but the meeting is not a synthesizing one; it "jars two hemispheres," but it does not answer the question that the "moon-eyed fishes" asked in stanza V: "What does this vaingloriousness down here?" The iceberg is the efficient cause of the ship sinking, but for Hardy there is no final cause, and the answer is only a recognition that there are no answers.

The "Convergence" is an example of the discovery in a public event of a situation which Hardy more often saw in personal, human terms—the disastrous accident which shouldn't have happened but did, "the ill-judged execution of the well-judged plan of things." He made the similarity to his more personal situations more striking by setting the convergence in terms of sexual union: *couches, ravish, mate, consummation* make of the collision a kind of cosmic mismarriage (marriage in Hardy is almost invariably a paradigm of his antinomial vision of the world, a symbol of the destructive interaction of opposites).

In spite of the presence of the Immanent Will there is no philosophy in the "Convergence"; there is only Hardy's sense of the inscrutable universal irony of things. It is a good poem, good because it is ironic and not philosophical, for Hardy's home-made philosophy usually betrayed him in his verse, while his ironic sense was his greatest poetic asset. Irony gave him what background or conventional belief might have provided a more traditional-minded poet—a formal pattern and a method of restraint. Rationalism had deprived him of inherited values, and had left him a world in which experience could not be given order by relation to a received system. By seeing an event in terms of its opposite, Hardy gave it a significance independent of external reference; by setting two views of the event in juxtaposition he gave his poems form.

Irony also provided him with a defense against his greatest potential weakness—sentimentality. A sensitive man, aware of suffering and injustice in the world and lacking a traditional justification or explanation of them, is prone to an excessive reaction—the response to evil, when not balanced by a conviction of good, may be manifested in uncontrolled emotion. A purely literary tradition might have provided a classically trained poet with a sufficient restraint; but Hardy had not even that support. He had only the bare facts of his own observation, experience without referent. The antinomial pattern set a possible, if not always sufficient, curb to his compassion.

Like other antinomial modes of expression (Yeats's, for example, or the early Eliot's), Hardy's was not always equal to the poetic occasion; sometimes it distorted or restricted the material submitted to it. The restrictiveness of the pattern is most easily seen in Hardy's choice of situations. Certain situations are obviously easily adaptable to ironic statement, and Hardy had a few which he used again and again. The Return, for instance, is one of his favorites: a person thought dead returns to those who thought him so, a husband returns to his unfaithful wife, a mature man to his childhood sweetheart, a long-absent traveler to his home village, the dead to scenes and persons from their pasts. Usually the return is to the past, and the irony is in the resulting disparity between expectation and reality.

One can see why the Return was an action which appealed to Hardy; it symbolizes man's efforts to reverse the movement of Time, and to assert the present existence of the past. And, as Hardy treated it, it symbolizes man's failure to do so. For while Hardy recognized the will to do so as a part of human nature, he also recognized the futility of the effort: universal nature takes no notice of man's will, and in the conflict between universal nature and human nature, the Immanent Will always wins. In the world as Hardy saw it, Time is a one-directional and non-reversible process, implying mutability and mortality, and thus inevitably defeating man in his struggles for permanence and order. Hardy's Time is a destructive, never a curative force, and it cannot be transcended (Hardy does not find hope of immortality, as Shakespeare did in his sonnets, either in the continuation of the race or in the timeless work of art or in the immortal soul).

This obsession with Time is one important aspect of Hardy's philosophy, but it also has a structural dimension. Hardy most commonly organized his poems in temporal terms, rather than in spatial or logical forms: that is to say, he ordered his actions by relating them in time, and not in space or in the terms of a syllogism. *Meaning* is a function, not of experience itself or of reason, but of retrospection. Hardy was, as the notebooks and poems indicate again and again, a hoarder of events. He seemed to hold on to even the most trivial or apparently meaningless experience, just in case it might reveal its meaning later. He was a great hand at recalling anniversaries—"On this day ten years ago I last saw . . ." or "I first met," or "X died"—and at remembering trivial events from the distant past. A number of poems show this curious intimacy with the remote past very clearly: "In Time of 'The Breaking of Nations,' " for example, was written in 1914 from an experience of 1870; and "Louisa in the Lane," a poem based on a casual childhood association, was written in the last year of his life.

In almost every case, however, the point of view of the poem is not the moment in the past, but a present from which the past can be viewed ironically, sadly, nostalgically. Both the theme and the structure are provided by Time. Usually this time-structure takes the form of a simple two-term opposition of past and present, before and after. This opposition frequently appears even in the titles: "Her Death and After," "The Coquette and After," "Before Life and After," "Before and After Summer," "First Sight of Her and After," "Before Marching and After."

The most obvious danger in so simple and bare a structure is that it may become a mechanical, drop-the-other-shoe system, in which every apparently happy, good event is inevitably contradicted by a succeeding event. In "He Fears His Good Fortune" Hardy's speaker, surrounded by radiance and sweetness, thinks, "I've no claim

> ... to be thus crowned:
> I am not worthy this:—
> Must it not go amiss?—
> Well . . . let the end foreseen
> Come duly!—I am serene."
> —And it came.
>
> (*Collected Poems*, p. 479)

And it always *does* come in Hardy; but not always in ways which seem organic and necessary to the poetic situation. An example of a mechanical reversal which doesn't work is the little poem, "The Lodging-House Fuchsias":

> Mrs. Masters's fuchsias hung
> Higher and broader, and brightly swung,
>   Bell-like, more and more
> Over the narrow garden-path,
> Giving the passer a sprinkle-bath
>   In the morning.
>
> She put up with their pushful ways,
> And made us tenderly lift their sprays,
>   Going to her door:
> But when her funeral had to pass
> They cut back all the flowery mass
>   In the morning.
>
> <div align="right">(<i>Winter Words</i>, p. 44)</div>

The irony here is too easy. We are asked to feel that the juxtaposition of the two visits ("us" and the funeral) expresses something amiss in the nature of things—Mrs. Masters was tender, but Death is not—something like that; yet such a criticism of existence is scarcely inherent in either the death or the cutting back of the flowers. Nor is there any clear significance in the repetition of "in the morning"; the phrase ties the two stanzas together in a mechanical way, and asserts an ironic relationship between them which does not in fact exist. All in all, the poem asks of us a greater emotional response to the mere *fact* of mortality than we are likely to give. To Hardy, of course, the fact was all that there was; his poetry is, to use a current phrase, "the poetry of experience," not the poetry of values. But in this instance, and in many other poems like it, the experience has not been significantly ordered.

Although the simple before-and-after organization of "The Lodging-House Fuchsias" is Hardy's most characteristic structural device, he occasionally arranged the action of a poem sequentially, in the series of related steps, so as to give a pesudo-logical form to the poetic event. Of these sequential poems, " 'Ah, Are You Digging?' " is probably the best; certainly it is the most anthologized. In this poem, as in others similarly organized (for example, "Heiress and Architect," "Memory and I," "The Five Students"), an initial situation is stripped of the values implicit in it, one at a time, until in the end there is left only the bare, denying reality. The speaker of " 'Ah, Are You Digging?' " a dead woman, inquires after the affections which have survived her, and by which she lives in those who remember her. She is denied in turn the attentions of lover, kin, enemy, and faithful dog; the grave, as the dog tells her, is a place to bury bones, not affections.

Such a sequential structure is not inherently weak—in popular ballads, from which it no doubt derives, it is often highly effective. But there is a danger implicit in it of making the sequence mechanical rather than necessary, an arbitrary series of steps from appearance (first stanza) to reality (last stanza). In " 'Ah, Are Your Digging?' " a single ironic reversal of expectation is repeated in a descending order of deprivations. Once the downward movement is established the end becomes inevitable and the irony becomes gross and automatic. The whole ironic structure of the poem rests upon a single assertion—that no affection survives death, neither love nor hate, nor even the devotion of dumb beasts. This assertion is, in the first place, not true (as Hardy himself demonstrated in his poems to his dead wife, and even to his dead pets); certainly it is neither true nor effective in the terms in which it is offered in the poem. Irony, elsewhere in Hardy a fine and delicate instrument for the creation of complex awarenesses, is here clumsy and cynical, and close to the kind of pseudo-ironic sentimentality that one finds so often in Housman, and so rarely in Hardy.

When set with the philosophical poems, Hardy's sequential poems invite the conclusion that he was weakest when he attempted to find meaning in experience through logical, developmental patterns, and strongest when he was content simply to set life's contrarieties together and let them act upon one another. Existence as he understood it resisted organization—the universe seemed "a half-expressed, an ill-expressed idea"[27]—and he was left with a single pattern which alone did no violence to his vision. That in spite of such a limitation he yet managed to write the number of fine poems he did is admirable, and astonishing. Any canon of those fine poems will inevitably consist of poems antinomial in structure; as a criterion for judgment the antinomial pattern is generally a trustworthy one for dealing with Hardy.

Hardy was, as John Crowe Ransom observed, "extremely ingenious and experienced in catching fresh perceptions of his brutal fact."[28] Because the fact was essentially only *one* fact—that experience contradicts itself and ultimately denies generalizations about values—not all of the perceptions were fresh nor equally apposite to it. Some poems fail through staleness, the sense one has that Hardy has said this better somewhere else, and some through radical irrelevance, the sense that unsuitable material has been forced into a shape dictated by the desire to elevate the "brutal fact" into a philosophy. Where the philosophy is most apparent, the failure is likely to be the greatest, for Hardy's thought was a ponderous and rigid burden. But where the perception is fresh, the occasion adequate, and the philosophy submerged in irony, the poems succeed in capturing what

Hardy once set as his goal—"the *other side* of common emotions" (*Early Life,* p. 76).

If we say, then, that Hardy was a philosophical poet, we must do so cautiously. Certainly he tried hard to be one, and only if we are conscious of the force of that effort can we see clearly the fundamental qualities of his poetry. But we must also recognize that his struggle toward the level of generalizations about belief failed, and that the philosophy exists in the good poems as a direction of effort, a yearning, rather than as a realized system. In the end we must settle for what we have—not a philosophy, but a body of poetry which at its best expresses in irony what Hardy's philosophy could not comprehend—his sense of the irreconcilable disparity between the way things ought to be and the way they are: the failure of the universe to answer man's need for order.

4

The Hardy Style

UNFAVORABLE JUDGMENTS of Hardy's poetry have generally been of two kinds: either philosophical or stylistic. The philosophy has been criticized either because it is wicked—the "village atheist" school of Chesterton—or because it gets in the way of the poetry (Hardy, says R. P. Blackmur, was a "sensibility violated by ideas"[29]). The style has been criticized either because it is not poetic, or because it does not exist.

Maugham described it, writing of his transparent Edward Driffield:

He was for long thought to write very bad English, and indeed he gave you the impression of writing with the stub of a blunt pencil; his style was laboured, an uneasy mixture of the classical and the slangy, and his dialogue was such as could never have issued from the mouth of a human being.[30]

Although this passage is meant to describe the novels, it applies as well to a common view of the poems, a view which began with the first reviewers of Hardy's verse, and which still continues. In those early reviews, certain points were made again and again: Hardy's rhythms were prosaic, "arbitrarily irregular," "clumsy"; his language was "needlessly inflated," "persistently clumsy," "unexciting and unpoetic"; his range was narrow and monotonous. Even a reviewer as perceptive and sympathetic as Lytton Strachey gave his approval in a curiously left-handed way: "It is full of poetry," Strachey wrote of *Satires of Circumstance,* "and yet it is also full of ugly and cumbrous expressions, clumsy metres, and flat, prosaic turns of speech."[31] It was, one perhaps had to admit, poetry; but it was certainly not poetic. "Poetry is not his medium," *The Spectator* concluded. "He is not at home, he does not move easily in it.... Mr. Hardy is a master of fiction, but not a master of music." And the *Saturday Review* added, somewhat more generously: "So far as it is possible to be a poet without having a singing voice, Mr. Hardy is a poet, and a profoundly interesting one."[32]

Any reader of Hardy's poetry must recognize that some of these judgments, at least, are just. Hardy's poems do seem awkward, halting, and often ungrammatical. The language ranges from the dialectal to the technical, and is full of strange, tongue-twisting coinages. The sentences move crab-wise across the page, or back toward the subject of the verb: "They know Earth-secrets that know not I," a characteristic poem ends. And there are awkward inversions, which Hardy carried to greater lengths than any other poet writing in English. For example, there is the last line of this stanza from "At a Bridal":

> Should I, too, wed as slave to Mode's decree,
> And each thus found apart, of false desire,
> A stolid line, whom no high aims will fire
> As had fired ours could ever have mingled we ....
>
> (*Collected Poems,* p. 8)

These are the things we think of when we think of the typical Hardy style; and they are all there in the poems.

But in justice to Hardy we must add two substantial qualifications to this idea of his style: that his poems are not *all* awkwardness, and that awkwardness, like the melodiousness which he does not have, may be functional in the poem.

The first point, because it is the easiest, we will consider first. It is a simple fact that, quantitatively speaking, Hardy is syntactically and grammatically orthodox more often than not. Many of the best poems are almost conversational in style, and do little violence to prose syntax or to the rules of grammar. "A Broken Appointment" is a slight, but entirely successful example of this kind of poem:

> You did not come,
> And marching Time drew on, and wore me numb.—
> Yet less for loss of your dear presence there
> Than that I thus found lacking in your make
> That high compassion which can overbear
> Reluctance for pure lovingkindness' sake
> Grieved I, when, as the hope-hour stroked its sum,
> You did not come.
>
> You love not me,
> And love alone can lend you loyalty;
> —I know and knew it. But, unto the store
> Of human deeds divine in all but name,
> Was it not worth a little hour or more
> To add yet this: Once you, a woman, came
> To soothe a time-torn man; even though it be
> You love not me.
>
> (*Collected Poems*, p. 124)

One recognizes at once that this is a Hardy poem; but "clumsy," "awkward," and "prosaic" are not the right terms to describe its distinctive style. In form it is an answer to the "blunt pencil" view of Hardy's art. The stanza is a fairly involved one: Hardy uses it with grace, adjusting long sentences to the rhyme scheme easily and employing inversion to make the rhyme only once. Its ease is not quite the ease of prose speech—Hardy always insists on the essential formality of poetry, on what Patmore described as "the necessity of manifesting, as well as moving in, the bonds of verse"[33]—but this is true of conventional poetry in general, and describes nothing peculiar to Hardy.

It might be easier to define Hardy's style negatively, in terms of what it is not. First of all, it is not melodious or "lyric" in any conventional sense—only the most tedious (and least typical) of Hardy's poems can be said to sing. His characteristic pace is erratic and abrupt, the pace of thoughtful speech or of spoken thought. In "A Broken Appointment" this pace is to a considerable extent a function of the syntax, which is slow and involved in the first stanza, and is broken by many stops in the second. The syntax is not particularly odd, and it is not, as it often is in Auden and Eliot and even Shakespeare, ambiguous—one can always establish in Hardy's verse what modifies what. Only one phrase, "Grieved I," stands out as a violation of normal order, because, although it is the main clause of the sentence, it is held off for four lines, and because it is inverted where the meter does not require inversion. The withholding of the admission of grief implies a relationship which is common in Hardy—the personal response is consistently subordinated to the situation, the "I" is introduced modestly, almost apologetically, into an external scene which is the thing in the poem that really matters (in this Hardy is the antithesis of the Romantic poet, who uses the external world as a reflector of himself). As for the unnecessary inversion, one finds it often in Hardy—it is one way of reminding the reader, after a passage of easy prose syntax, that the poem is still operating within "the bonds of verse."

Another element in the poem which affects the pace is its sheer oral difficulty; it is hard to read, and impossible to read musically. Hardy rarely uses sound to smooth his poetic texture, but rather, as here, to roughen it (try reading aloud "Than that I thus found lacking in your make"). The same is true of his arrangement of stresses; though the over-all pattern is generally regular, the exact location of stresses may be puzzling in spots, especially where the compound words of which Hardy was so fond leave the stress hovering over two or three syllables. This oral roughness has led some critics to conclude that he had no ear; but rather, I think, he heard a different kind of music, and a kind which should not sound strange to the modern reader's ear—it is not so different, after all, from the dissonances of Meredith and Patmore and Hopkins, or, for that matter, of Pound and Eliot.

"A Broken Appointment" offers no really outlandish examples of Hardy's peculiarities of diction. There are no neologisms (unless you count "lovingkindness" and "hopehour"), no dialectal or archaic words, nothing to stumble over. Yet the poem is typical in this respect, that from it one can infer no norm of diction—all language, abstract and particular, fresh and trite, old and new, is equally available to the poet (we will return to the question of Hardy's diction in more detail in Chapter Six).

At this point we can say, then, of Hardy's style that it is assertively unmusical and often harsh, and that this harshness is a function of the manipulation of syntax, sound, and diction so as to defeat lyric fluidity and to restrict the movement of the verse to a slow, uneven, often uncertain pace.

The question of the way in which this style can be regarded as functional in the poems remains. The answer lies, I think, in the quality which Hardy praised in Barnes: "closeness of phrase to his vision."

The vision in Hardy's case is, as I said in the last chapter, "his sense of the irreconcilable disparity between the way things ought to be and the way they are: the failure of the universe to answer man's need for order." That failure is a constant in Hardy's writing; and because of that failure the idea of poetic order is a very different thing for Hardy from what it was for his predecessors. Hardy says in "In Tenebris," "if way to the Better there be, it exacts a full look at the Worst." The "worst" is suffering, mortality, change, death—all meaningless in a meaningless, indifferent universe. Hardy did not try to reconcile man to his predicament, or to resolve the evident disparities and contradictions of existence—he merely recorded them: he was, as he put it, "humbly recording diverse readings of [life's] phenomena as they are forced upon us by chance and change" (*Collected Poems,* p. 75). The "worst" was the actual phenomenal world, the way things are. Like other modern poets (notably Pound in the *Cantos* and William Carlos Williams), Hardy restricted himself largely to his vision of the actual, a poetic world without abstract ideals or absolutes, and strove for "closeness of phrase" to that vision.

One result, and this is also true to some degree of the other poets mentioned, was an uncompromising fidelity to fact and detail ("Oh, but it really happened" was, for him, a valid defense of a poem). One cannot read far in Hardy's poems without noticing the precision of observation, the command of minute detail. Sometimes there is nothing more and the poem seems merely trivial, a description, or more often, since Hardy's method was primarily dramatic, an anecdote; but often detail and vision fuse and support each other, and the poem succeeds. "A January Night" succeeds in this way, because detail precedes vision and prepares us for it:

> The rain smites more and more,
> The east wind snarls and sneezes;
> Through the joints of the quivering door
>   The water wheezes.
>
> The tip of each ivy-shoot
> Writhes on its neighbour's face:
> There is some hid dread afoot
>   That we cannot trace.
>
> Is it the spirit astray
> Of the man at the house below
> Whose coffin they took in to-day?
>   We do not know.
>
>   (*Collected Poems*, p. 438)

This is a very characteristic poem, in that all we are allowed to *know* is the substantive situation—the wind, the rain, and the writhing ivy. The dread is in what we do not and cannot know, the forces or the emptiness behind the actual. The poem does not explain anything, nor does it set this particular experience in the context of any system of belief; rather it dramatizes man's *inability* to explain, his ignorance and his horror.

    Man's ignorance, and his inability to reduce the universe to significant order, are the principal factors in Hardy's vision, and in his poetry. One result, as we might expect, is a style built upon tensions and disparities. These tensions and disparities function in many ways: form against idea, prose syntax against metrical necessity, one level of diction against another, image against image, or image against abstraction. The poetic materials are likely to be heterogeneous, and their combinations apparently whimsical—one rarely feels in Hardy's verse the force of poetic decorum at work. This is odd if one considers the Victorian decorousness of the man, but not strange in the light of his thought. For Hardy's thought, while it had not achieved a system of belief, had freed him from traditional belief, and with this philosophical freedom went a poetical freedom as great, and as empty. Chance rules Hardy's universe, and often it seems to determine his style as well. And why, after all, in a lawless universe should there be laws governing poetry? Why *not* make poems out of clashing incongruities, since this is the way the world is?

This argument seems to lead us to the conclusion that Hardy's poems are good or bad by accident, that he did not really have control of his medium. This critical conclusion did persist throughout Hardy's poetic career, and he was understandably annoyed by it: "The reviewer," he complained, "so often supposes that where Art is not visible it is unknown to the poet under criticism. Why does he not think of the art of concealing art?" (*Later Years,* p. 184).

The notion that the machinery and the effort of creation should not be visible in the final work is not an uncommon one—Yeats says much the same thing in "Adam's Curse." But Hardy seems to mean something more here. In his aesthetic (insofar as he had one), "art" usually means the technical finish, the conventions operating within a work; in the remark quoted above he seems to be saying that *his* intention is to eliminate convention from the surface of his work. The acceptance of conventions implies the acceptance of the idea of order which produced them; like other late

Victorians Hardy was driven by his rejection of inherited beliefs to a rejection of inherited poetic methods and to a search for new ones. "There is no new poetry," he wrote in his notebook, "but the new poet—if he carry the flame on further (and if not he is no new poet)—comes with a new note. And that new note it is that troubles the critical waters" (*Later Years,* p. 78). The "new note," he makes clear, is the voice of his thought: style is a metaphor for belief.

Like Donne, Hardy was profoundly disturbed by a "new philosophy," and like Donne he found in a harsh and jagged style a way of transforming his disturbance into poetry. His gifts were less than Donne's, his intellect less tough, and so the results are less often successful poems. But the relation of style to thought is much the same, and is based on the same perception—that a breakdown of beliefs invalidates the conventional styles in which those beliefs were expressed, and that at such a time the artist, if he is to be true to his vision of reality, must find a personal style for his personal vision.

Hardy defined *style* in his essay, "The Profitable Reading of Fiction":

Style, as far as the word is meant to express something more than literary finish, can only be treatment, and treatment depends upon the mental attitude of the novelist; thus entering into the very substance of a narrative, as into that of any other kind of literature. A writer who is not a mere imitator looks upon the world with his personal eyes, and in his peculiar moods; thence grows up his style, in the full sense of the term ... Those who would profit from the study of style should formulate an opinion of what it consists in by the aid of their own educated understanding, their perception of natural fitness, true and high feeling, sincerity, unhampered by considerations of nice collocation and balance of sentences, still less by conventionally accepted examples (*Life and Art,* p. 71).

This is, in its essentials, a standard romantic treatment of literary values. The attitudes of the artist—his "sincerity," his "true and high feeling"—are what matter; the literary tradition is hampering convention, and the verbal surface of the poem is mere "literary finish." The trouble, of course, is that if you take away the tradition and the literary finish there is nothing left; the most exquisite feeling depends upon words and conventional forms for objective existence. But Hardy never seemed to see this; in his aesthetic, technique was rigorously separated from and subordinated to thought, and thought in turn was a private, almost solipsistic, act. One finds, scattered through his notes, remarks like this: "My weakness has always been to prefer the large intention of an unskillful artist to the trivial intention of an accomplished one: in other words, I am more interested in the high ideas of a feeble executant than in the high execution of a feeble thinker" (*Later Years,* pp. 90-91). Surely few modern critics would consider this separation of the artist into thinker and executant a realistic one, but apparently for Hardy it was a necessary distinction.

It was necessary, I think, because it could be made into a kind of declaration of independence—independence both from traditional systems of belief which he could not accept, and from the stylistic conventions which he associated with those beliefs. Hardy's poet is a man alone with his "mental attitudes" and those attitudes are his only guide, the only fit object of his fidelity. Consequently, when he defines *style,* he does so in terms which most critics would probably think more properly defined *tone,* a considerably narrower critical concept. By making style identical with tone, Hardy points up two important and related qualities of his verse—the distinctive personal voice, and the consistently personal point of view. Belief, and the lonely believer, are the coordinates of his poetic reality. Thus a conventional poetic act, a striving after a "nice collocation and balance of sentences" is an act of infidelity, and a harsh and personal tone the mark of a true heart.

Hardy tried, as I remarked earlier, to write monistic poetry—poetry, that is, in which the actual is the only reality, and in which there is no other, invisible world above and beyond the actual, to which the things in a poem refer and from which they derive significance and value. Such a position, consistently held, would seem to have certain necessary effects on a poet's style: he would not use symbols to make reality visible, since only the visible *is* real; he would avoid metaphor for the same reason—metaphor implies that two obviously different objects or events partake in a common reality; he would rather favor direct description, in which a hawk is a hawk and not a handsaw, or similes, which assert the discreteness of the elements involved.

This, in fact, does describe Hardy's practice pretty well. He is neither a symbolic nor a metaphorical writer; in his poems things remain intransigently things. (In the two poems quoted in this chapter, for example, only the second line of "A Broken Appointment"—"And marching Time drew on, and wore me numb"—could be called metaphorical, and the metaphor there is mixed and vague.)

But Hardy apparently found the style proper to his belief, like the belief itself, inadequate. If the unseen reality could not come in the front door as philosophy, it could come in the back door as superstition; if it could not clothe itself in symbol and metaphor, it could appear as omen and abstraction—"our old friend Dualism," says Hardy, is "a tough old chap." Hence the phantoms, ghosts, and dreads in the poems; hence also the presence among the meticulous particulars of abstract words—Crass Casualty, Time, Change —and personifications of the sort that populate the Overworld of *The Dynasts*. These terms have one quality in common: they all refer to the dark, inexplicable side of existence. The superstitions in the poems are all frightening superstitions ("Signs and Tokens" catalogues some of these); the Overworld includes spirits of Pity, Irony and Rumour, but not of Happiness or Joy or Peace.

The tension between particular and abstraction may be spelled out (as in "Hap") or simply implied (as in "A January Night"); in either case, one area of language qualifies and casts doubt upon the other—they are, in other words, antinomial. This relationship does not, as metaphor does, imply a necessary relationship between the terms—it assumes no order. It simply points to an incompatibility in the nature of things. It is a fundamental stylistic manifestation of Hardy's vision.

We may see a further effect of this vision in the general flatness of Hardy's descriptive language. While description is often sharp and detailed, one rarely feels the shock of recognition that comes from seeing experience in a new light; the light is always the same—Hardy's twilight. He seems to select his modifiers carelessly, as though any syllable would do, and they are consequently often obvious or simply trite (adjectives like *dear, sweet,* and *fine* are among his favorites). Perhaps because things in Hardy's verse are always and only things, he depends for his poetic force more upon action than upon description, upon what things do rather than on what they are. This is just another way of saying what I have said before, that Hardy is essentially a dramatic poet.

Action in poetry may operate in two ways: through dramatic scenes and through the use of verbs and verbals. Hardy's poems are almost always scenic in this sense—figures in a landscape, meeting, speaking, parting, returning. Often the point of view is located outside the action, and the speaking voice is the ironic observer, who records what *he* said and what *she* said, and comments ironically on how wrong they were; this is essentially the relation of audience to actors. Other poems are dramatic in that they are set as dialogues, often with one voice that of God, Nature, or some other personification of the nature of things. Such situations enabled Hardy to identify the terms of his antinomies with individual characters, and thus to make dramatic the conflict between them.

A dependence on verbal action seems to follow logically from this emphasis on the dramatic; conflict is active, and it can best be established through language denoting action. It is not surprising that Hardy's most striking and original words and phrases tend to be verbs or words derived from verbs; of the 200-odd coined words in the *Collected Poems* half are verbals—words like *aftergrinds, downstairward, outskeleton, self-widowered, unadieu'd*.[34] Many of the barbarisms which have troubled Hardy's critics are simply verbs used as adjectives or nouns: *bleed, float, scan, shines*, for example, all do the work of nouns in the poems. Such coinages, like the superstitions, generally refer to the dark side of existence.

To demonstrate how Hardy's stylistic oddities *may* function to express his vision of the world is not to say that they always *do* function effectively. The ways in which they succeed, and the ways in which they fail, can best be seen by examining in some detail two typical poems—one relatively weak and one very good.

"IF IT'S EVER SPRING AGAIN"

(SONG)

If it's ever spring again,
    Spring again,
I shall go where went I when
Down the moor-cock splashed, and hen,
Seeing me not, amid their flounder,
Standing with my arm around her;
If it's ever spring again,
    Spring again,
I shall go where went I then.

If it's ever summer-time,
    Summer-time,
With the hay crop at the prime,
And the cuckoos—two—in rhyme,
As they used to be, or seemed to,
We shall do as long we've dreamed to,
If it's ever summer-time,
    Summer-time,
With the hay, and bees achime.

                          (*Collected Poems*, p. 563)

One can immediately point to a number of technical flaws in this poem: the multiple and awkward inversions and the comic *flounder-around her* rhyme in the first stanza, the padding in the second (there is no point to the parenthetical *two* in the thirteenth line or in the last three words of the fourteenth, and the final line is entirely filler). Cuckoos rhyme and bees chime to make the rhyme scheme, not because rhyming and chiming are natural to them. The device of repetition is overworked and ineffective; the last lines of the stanzas in particular are feeble as refrains. One may legitimately conclude that the general slackness and ineptness of the poem is simply the result of Hardy's taking on a musical form to which his talents were not equal. Such a form makes metrical demands which simply silence Hardy's characteristic tone of voice—it is striking here that the metrical norm is dominant throughout the poem, and that diction and syntax are wrenched and padded to fit it, whereas in his best poems the opposite is more likely to be the case.

But such a conclusion does not get to the heart of the poem's weakness. The fundamental failure is a failure of tension; the poem is not antinomial, and in the absence of his principal formal element, Hardy goes slack. Dramatically, the poem is all *then;* the *now* is implicit in the title, but it has no existence in the poem itself. We do not see the rustic beatitude of spring and summer in contrast to anything; as observers we have nothing to stand on. Nor do the words themselves work upon each other to produce tensions; the language is entirely the language of conventional bucolic bliss, unqualified by the irony that the actual imposes. The nostalgia which suffuses the poem has no clear origin, and so remains gratuitous and sentimental.

As a contrast to this failure, we may consider one of Hardy's finest poems, "Bereft":

> In the black winter morning
> No light will be struck near my eyes
> While the clock in the stairway is warning
> For five, when he used to rise.
> Leave the door unbarred,
> The clock unwound.
> Make my lone bed hard—
> Would 'twere underground!

> When the summer dawns clearly,
> And the appletree-tops seem alight,
> Who will undraw the curtains and cheerly
> Call out that the morning is bright?
>
> When I tarry at market
> No form will cross Durnover Lea
> In the gathering darkness, to hark at
> Grey's Bridge for the pit-pat o' me.
>
> When the supper crock's steaming,
> And the time is the time of his tread,
> I shall sit by the fire and wait dreaming
> In a silence as of the dead.
> > Leave the door unbarred,
> > The clock unwound,
> > Make my lone bed hard—
> > Would 'twere underground!
>
> (*Collected Poems*, pp. 192-93)

Like "If It's Ever Spring Again," this is a memory poem, but there the similarity ends. "Bereft," though it employs a fairly involved stanza form, is not "musical"—the voice speaks in the accents of despair, not of melodious nostalgia. As in so many of Hardy's poems, the principal tension lies in the relation of past and present, but in this case we know exactly what each term implies. The past means *order*, especially the orderly relating of time and action; the speaker is the kind of woman who says, "There's a right time for everything." We find this assumption in each stanza of the poem (excepting the refrain, which images the present); when "he" was alive, life was a series of pleasing and appropriate actions—rising in the morning, supper at night, and a bed that was not lone and hard. Even the rhythms of these passages "keep time." The present, in contrast, is existence without order, time without its appropriate action—the clock has run down. The rhythms are uneven, out of time.

The images in the poem are individually flat and undecorated, the modifiers ordinary, the verbs exact and literal. As in many of Hardy's poems, there is little metaphorical use of imagery. The poem depends rather on the manipulation of carefully selected details—dark and light, the furnishings of a cottage, a few homely references to the world outside—which can be taken quite literally. Through these details a physical setting is created which is detailed and actual; the grieving widow has a context, and from the context we infer her character—neat, orderly, diligent, methodical. Because this context exists so precisely, the refrain can work powerfully against it without metaphor or other emotive heightening. The unbarred door, the unwound clock are, in the speaker's world, highly charged symbols of her loss, which is the loss of the ordering force in her life. But without the carefully composed literal world of the poem, the symbols would have little power to move us.

The world of the poem is not, of course, a product of the imagery alone. Rhythm also has its role, as I have suggested, and so does diction. The language is plain and unadorned, almost colloquial (but with a touch of the dialectal, perhaps, in *cheerly* and *tarry*); it is suitable both to the speaker and to the occasion.

We respond to the poem, or we accept what it says about grief, then, because it has, through the integrity of its imagery, its rhythms, and its language, "proved" to us that that grief is real. By giving us the world of the speaker's past in its bare actuality, Hardy has justified the burden of his refrain and has made a poem which is moving and beautiful.

These examples suggest that while Hardy's style was often an effective medium for the expression of his personal vision, it was severely limited in range. This limitation is essentially the limitation of his vision, for in Hardy style and belief were one. He could not write poems of song or celebration—in his experience he found nothing to sing about and nothing to celebrate. He could neither reason nor argue in verse, and the occasions on which he tried—his "philosophical" poems—were disastrous. Certain themes and certain aspects of experience were closed to him: religion was something other people believed in, love was only available to him as a theme when it was either betrayed or past, sex was cruelty but never ecstasy, and human happiness was a delusion or a memory made bitter by the unhappy present. Art, politics, urban life—all common themes among his successors—he ignored; his world was the dark side of Wessex, and it was there that he succeeded as a poet.

But Wessex is a private country, and its accent is private, too; if he achieved "closeness of phrase to his vision" there, it was *his* vision, and no one else's. So, though it is striking, it is perhaps inevitable that so fine a poet as Hardy has had virtually no influence on twentieth-century poetic style. Like Hopkins, he can be imitated, but his style is too personal, too eccentric to be used. Later poets, notably Auden and Dylan Thomas, have expressed their admiration for Hardy's poetry, but the mark of it is discernible in Auden only in his early schoolboy verse, and in Thomas not at all. Hardy died as a poet, as he died as a man, without heirs.

5

The Search for a Form

TURNING FROM the question of style to the question of form, we can take at least one idea with us. Hardy was, as I have said, anti-formalist in his aesthetic; he insisted that "in a work of art it is the accident which *charms,* not the intention; *that* we only like and admire" (*Early Life,* p. 251), and he consistently subordinated technique to thought in his own critical judgments. In discussing Hardy's style I suggested that this anti-formalist bias might be regarded as an aspect of Hardy's sense of his radical isolation from the intellectual and poetic tradition: if the traditional beliefs are dead, then the artistic process becomes a continual starting over. If this is true of Hardy's style, we might expect that it would also be true of the poetic forms he used—they should be personal and eccentric in something like the same way.

At first glance this does seem to be the case. It is quite true, as Edmund Gosse remarked in his appreciation of Hardy's poetry, that "his stanzaic invention is abundant; no other Victorian poet, not even Swinburne, has employed so many forms, mostly of his own invention. . . ." But we may question the rest of Gosse's sentence: ". . . and employed them so appropriately, that is to say, in so close harmony with the subject or story enshrined in them."³⁵ There are, to be sure, a great many different metrical forms in Hardy's work, and many of them are "invented" stanzas, generally rather elaborate combinations of lines of various lengths, often rhymed in a complicated way. But these inventions are actually only variations on each other; the individual lines are usually conventionally iambic, with standard variations, and, given lines of from one to six feet and a great deal of patience, one could by permutations construct them all. They are not, in most cases, particularly appropriate to their subjects, and certainly Gosse's implication that Hardy was consistently capable of organic forms is quite inaccurate. It should be apparent (and one is surprised that it wasn't apparent to Hardy) that elaborate, irregular stanzas could not be appropriate for poems which have a strong dramatic or narrative aspect. For narrative requires a regular and unobtrusive metrical movement, while irregular lines in a stanza lay claim, by their very irregularity, to some special importance, and delay the movement. One asks, "Why did he make that line shorter, and that line longer?" The answer, in Hardy's case, is usually that there *is* no apparent reason, and even the best of his more elaborate "inventions" seem quite accidental, as though the receptacle had been constructed first, and then an idea had been dropped into it (one can't help recalling Mrs. Hardy's remark about "verse skeletons").

The point here is that in Hardy's poems a relation between form and idea exists which is different from that which we assume in most contemporary poets. As John Hollander recently observed, "It is possible . . . to speak of Hardy's *choice of meter* in a way that we would be reluctant to do in the case of Hopkins, Eliot, Pound or Yeats, and, even more, to pass judgment on that choice by designating it an arbitrary one."[36] For Hardy, that is, the inseparability of form and content, which we set so much store by, simply did not exist. We know that on the one hand he often wrote his poems in prose, and later versified them, and on the other that he composed "verses" of nonsense syllables, to be filled in later. Metrical form was not something which grew up organically with the poem but was rather a framework or a mold, having an existence independent of its content, a view which we might call, rather loosely, "traditional."

But at the same time, Hardy did not "choose a meter" in quite the same way that, say, Wordsworth did. For one thing, he chose a great many *more* meters, and used the traditional ones on the whole with less authority, and for another, he put bits and pieces of meter together to compose his own stanzas. He evidently had little sense of the "emblematic" aspect of meter—the associations which have, through traditional usage, gathered around certain forms like the sonnet and the ballad. Consequently, his sonnets are often untraditional in content, while his ballads are untraditional in meter.

Hardy *was* traditional, however, in this: he clearly regarded choosing a meter as a kind of contract, which, once entered into, was not to be broken. The choice was apparently often a matter simply of getting one stanza written; the rest of the idea was then pressed into units of the same form. Frequently this process took a long time, and it may provide one explanation for the long gestation periods of some of Hardy's poems. The evidence of Hardy's revisions suggests that once he had committed himself to a stanza he did not question the wisdom of that commitment—we will return to this point when we examine

Hardy's revisions in Chapter Eight—and he did not allow himself irregularities beyond rather narrow limits. I have quoted above (p. 20) a passage on this point from the *Later Years,* in which Mrs. Hardy discusses, in a voice which is pretty clearly Hardy's own, the reception of the *Wessex Poems.* The claim which this passage makes for freedom of form is a radical one, and the poet who realized it would be a considerable innovator. But the examples of "cunning irregularity" which are offered—metrical pause, reversed beats, stress-count—are those which most traditional English poets have felt free to use, and it is hard to see how they make Hardy's poetry any more Gothic than Shakespeare's is. In a few poems, such as "In Sherborne Abbey," Hardy does use an extremely asymmetrical form, but in this case the "Gothicness" seems a function of the subject (Hardy was the sort of poet who would feel that a poem set in an abbey required a Gothic form). In general, he did not deviate from a set stanzaic form once he had committed himself to it.

There are, to be sure, a few poems in which the verse form changes radically and effectively. "The Voice" is an example:

> Woman much missed, how you call to me, call to me,
> Saying that now you are not as you were
> When you had changed from the one who was all to me,
> But as at first, when our day was fair.
>
> Can it be you that I hear? Let me view you, then,
> Standing as when I drew near to the town
> Where you would wait for me: yes, as I knew you then,
> Even to the original air-blue gown!
>
> Or is it only the breeze, in its listlessness
> Travelling across the wet mead to me here,
> You being ever dissolved to wan wistlessness,
> Heard no more again far or near?

> Thus I; faltering forward,
> Leaves around me falling,
> Wind oozing thin through the thorn from norward,
> And the woman calling.
>
> <div align="right">(<i>Collected Poems</i>, pp. 325-26)</div>

We have here, as we usually have in Hardy, a poem composed in antinomial terms: present is set against past, life against death, hope against despair. The poem is unusual, however, in that the distinction between the terms is most striking in its metrical aspect. Hardy was usually content to continue in the stanza form in which he began, but here he uses a change of form for significant effect. The first three stanzas are set in the triple rhythm which Hardy used frequently, but not often very well. The rhythm is at first fairly mellifluous—the first stanza scans easily without any serious problems—but becomes rougher in the third stanza, with extra syllables and juxtaposed stresses. The final stanza, the "Present" term of the poem, is set in an altogether different meter, which "falters forward" irregularly, as the speaker does.

"The Voice" is an excellent poem, and a part of its excellence lies in its use of metrical irregularity; still, one must admit that the metrical trick is a somewhat mechanical one, a single change of gear to represent a change of circumstance. It is of course very characteristic of Hardy's antinomial habits of mind that two forward speeds were sufficient: what we have here is simply an example of the "pattern" in its metrical aspect. But to a reader familiar with metrical experimentation of the last fifty years, Hardy's venture into organic form must seem a rather timid one, which did not stray very far from metrical traditionalism.

All in all, Hardy's relation to the prosodic tradition of English poetry is an ambivalent one. He shared with the more radical innovators of his time a certain experimental spirit, but he was both less extreme and less programmatic than they. Hopkins had his "sprung rhythm," Patmore the "catalytic" meters of his odes, Bridges his "loose Alexandrines"; but Hardy, though he invented stanzas, never ventured far from the iambic norm which had been the standard English rhythm for four centuries. Perhaps he was metrically less radical than the others because he was a more self-taught poet; whatever the reason, he did have a naïve reverence for, or at least a dependence on, the forms which he inherited. He did not have the art to make a totally new technique (as Hopkins, and later Eliot did); like that recurrent figure in his poems, The Returner, he kept coming back to tradition, only to find that he didn't belong there, or that it wasn't as he remembered it. He spent his life seeking a form appropriate to his vision, but he never found it.

A substantial amount of Hardy's verse is set in traditional metrical forms, and even his great experiment, *The Dynasts,* is in large part composed of units in traditional meters. Hardy was apparently proud of his achievements in these forms: Ford Madox Ford recalled that at a week-end house-party Hardy "talked—after sufficient pressing—by the hour about *The Dynasts,* going over page after page minutely in a nook on the beach, explaining why he had used here heroics, here Alcaics or Sapphics or ballad forms or forms invented by himself, explaining how such and such an incident had been suggested to him ... and keenly delighting in his achievement."[37] His achievement in the traditional meters was not, however, always as delightful as all that.

The blank verse of *The Dynasts,* for example, puts Hardy fairly low among what Zola called "Shakespeare's bastards" —it is workmanlike, but seldom more. The same might be said of his Shakespearian sonnets and of his ventures into various French forms. Hardy seems to have tried just about every metrical form that came his way, moving restlessly from one to another without staying with any one form for very long.

Thus far, when we have referred to "tradition" we have meant the literary tradition as expressed in the continuation of metrical forms from Chaucer to the present day. But in speaking of Hardy one must, of course, recognize another tradition—that generally called the "folk tradition." From this essentially non-literary tradition, Hardy's poetry derives some of its most personal characteristics. In Hardy's case, the folk-tradition breaks into two clear subdivisions which influenced Hardy's verse in quite distinct ways: popular ballads, and hymns and country songs.

One might expect that ballads and country songs would constitute a single metrical influence, but in fact this does not seem to be the case. Hardy's poems do very often resemble folk ballads, but the resemblances are in terms of tone, attitude, and dramatic structure, rather than in meter. In these terms, the ballads provide a prime analogy to Hardy's work. Hardy shared the ballad view of life—its violence, its fatality, and its indifference to man's desires. His notebooks are full of ballad-like anecdotes of love and death, which clearly carried great significance for him; and, when he first planned his masterpiece, *The Dynasts,* he saw it as a cycle of ballads (several of his poems seem to be remnants of this discarded scheme—"Valenciennes," "San Sebastian," "Leipzig," "The Peasant's Confession" all have

Napoleonic themes). This "ballad-view" is evident in most of his writing, certainly in the best of both prose and verse. His characters, both in the great Wessex novels and in the poems, move in a social void typical of the ballad world—the principals act alone, against a blank, dark backdrop. And his narrative method is the ballad method—the circumstances and the action are given barely; cause, motivation, and often results are left to the imagination, and the action is primal and violent. Certain of the short stories, particularly those collected in *Life's Little Ironies* under the title "A Few Crusted Characters," are in effect ballads in prose, and many of the poems which are not in ballad meter (and not many of the poems that he called ballads are) have the same sense of inexplicable catastrophe that one finds in "Lord Randal" and "The Twa Corbies."

If we talk about Hardy's formal debt to popular ballads, then, we must make clear that we mean *dramatic* form, and not *metrical* form. This dramatic form we find in even the most metrically eccentric of his "ballads." Each has a beginning, a middle, and an end, and the dramatic tension is as skillfully controlled as in a tragic play. At least one, "The Sacrilege," is subtitled "A Ballad-Tragedy"— others could be. It is not strange that Hardy considered putting "A Sunday Morning Tragedy" on the stage, and even "went so far as to shape the scenes, action, etc." (*Life and Art*, p. 128) before he abandoned the idea. For other poems he provided stage directions. He understood that the old ballads, like his modern ones, were essentially dramatic constructions; in a reply to criticism of *The Dynasts* he wrote:

... this play-shape is essentially if not quite literally, at one with the instinctive, primitive narrative shape. In legends and old ballads, in the telling of "an owre true tale" by countryfolk on winter nights over a dying fire, the place and time are briefly indicated at the beginning in almost all cases; and then the body of the story follows as what he said and what she said, the action being often suggested by the speeches alone. This likeness between the order of natural recital and the order of theatrical utility may be accidental; but there it is; and to write Scene so-and-so, time so-and-so instead of Once upon a time, At such a place, is a trifling variation that makes no difference to the mental images raised.[38]

Hardy's own sense of his relation to the ballad-tradition is clear enough; only the reasons are not. One would not expect a writer aware of the complex modern world to chose to align himself with a tradition which is, as Hardy says, instinctive and primitive, and which is extremely limited in range. But for Hardy these very limitations seem to have been attractive, or at least familiar—perhaps because they were his own.

In the passage quoted above, Hardy defines his "primitive narrative shape" in terms not of literary form, but of the handling of setting and action, and it is in these terms that the resemblance of Hardy's verse as a whole to traditional ballad literature is clearest. In the ballads, the narrator is detached, almost invisible, not involved: the action can be recorded dispassionately and without overt judgment (Hardy, you may remember, saw himself as "humbly recording" experience). Ballads focus on actions and on physical things—a knight, a white doe, a murder, a storm—not on the meanings of those events or the emotions appropriate to them. The actions are violent and inexplicable, as the world is; the things may be omens, but they retain their physical reality. The values involved are unspecified, or if specified are simple values like courage, fidelity, and endurance, which do not require a system of belief for their justification. The ballad world I have been describing is clearly the same world of minimal meaning that Hardy found himself caught in; the balladists, like Hardy, made their poems out of "the way things are," because there wasn't anything else to make them of.

If the ballads gave Hardy a dramatic form, popular music (both religious and secular) gave him metrical form. Hardy was a musician and a lover of music; in his youth he was a fiddler at country dances, and was familiar as well with the religious repertoire of instrumental "quires" like the Mellstock Quire in *Under the Greenwood Tree*. Throughout his life he was fond of English church-music— fond enough to attend frequently the services of a religion in which he did not believe; and he showed as well a continuing interest in and knowledge of country songs and dances. Such life-long associations with popular forms must have impressed them deeply into Hardy's mind—so deeply, perhaps, that long and common measure, and various song stanzas, naturally came to his mind when he sought for a lyric meter. At any rate he used the popular forms freely and easily, and on the whole to better effect than his own "invented" stanzas.

A habitual reference to popular religious and secular music would, one would expect, tend to undermine a poet's reverence for regularity, for both deviate from pattern in the interests of content. Many-versed songs of the public variety, like ballads and hymns, are predominantly stress-patterned; that is, the number of syllables will vary considerably from verse to verse, while the number of stresses per line remains constant (as in poems by Patmore and

Hopkins). Hopkins was aware of this relationship; in the "Author's Preface" to his *Poems* he wrote:

Sprung Rhythm is the most natural of things. For (1) it is the rhythm of common speech and of written prose, when rhythm is perceived in them. (2) It is the rhythm of all but the most monotonously regular music, so that in the words of choruses and refrains and in songs written closely to music it arises. (3) It is found in nursery rhymes, weather saws, and so on . . . .[39]

A poet schooled from childhood in these "public" forms would no doubt feel it his right to employ stress scansion where it suited his needs.

There is no evidence that Hardy developed this device into a theory, as Hopkins and Patmore did, but he did use it in a number of poems. If we examine the first stanza of "Bereft," for example, we will find that the number of syllables is irregular, but that the number of stresses per line is constant (with the exception of the sixth line).

	no. of syllables
In the bláck wínter mórning	7
No líght will be strúck near my éyes	8
While the clóck in the stáirway is wárning	10
For fíve, when he úsed to ríse.	7
Léave the dóor unbárred,	5
The clóck unwóund.	4
Máke my lóne bed hárd—	5
Wóuld 'twere undergróund.	5

This is less systematic than Hopkins' metrical experiments and seems, like many of Hardy's best effects, intuitive and accidental rather than contrived. Nevertheless, it works, and works in the way that ballads do.

When Hardy came, in his fifties, to consider publishing his poems, he made the following entry in his notebook: "Title:—'Songs of Five-and-Twenty Years'. Arrangement of the songs: Lyric Ecstasy inspired by music to have precedence" (*Later Years,* p. 3). He did not follow this plan in *Wessex Poems,* or indeed in any other volume, and it is difficult to associate "lyric ecstasy inspired by music" with any of the poems we know. The remark does indicate, however, the degree to which Hardy regarded himself as a "singer"; in the later volumes, in particular, there are many poems explicitly called songs, or subtitled "scherzando" or "nocturne" or "minor mode." Some of these seem to be songs only by fiat; they maintain the conversational, meditative tone and the irregular rhythms which are characteristic of Hardy's poetry. Others clearly have their metrical origins in musical rhythms. In one group particularly, the "set of country songs" in *Time's Laughingstocks,* Hardy seems to have drawn upon the rhythms of folk music for his meters, and these songs are on the whole graceful and pleasant, if not very important poems. But Hardy was not always successful in his uses of folk music; for example, "Timing Her," which carries the caption "Written to an old folk-tune," is a slack and awkward piece which suggests that Hardy was not equal to the demands of the verse form. In general, the more elaborate the musical form, the less likely Hardy was to work well within it.

The influence of hymns, though less explicit than that of folk music, is nevertheless pervasive. Hardy had a wide, scholarly knowledge of traditional church music, which he put to good use in the novels (in *Far From the Madding*

Crowd, Under the Greenwood Tree, and especially in the "Hundred-and-Ninth Psalm" episode in *The Mayor of Casterbridge*). But although he was familiar with most of the commonly used church music of his day, his appreciation of it was determinedly secular. Mrs. Hardy records the following letter from her husband to the editor of *The Review of Reviews*:

I am unable to answer your inquiry as to 'Hymns that have helped me'.

But the undermentioned have always been familiar and favourite hymns of mine *as poetry*:

1. 'Thou turnest man, O Lord, to dust'. Ps xc. *vv.* 3, 4, 5, 6. (Tate and Brady.)
2. 'Awake, my soul, and with the sun.' (Morning Hymn, Ken.).
3. 'Lead, kindly Light.' (Newman.)

(*Later Years,* p. 45. My italics)

"Tate and Brady" refers to *A New Version of the Psalms of David, Fitted to the Tunes used in Churches,* by Nahum Tate and Nicholas Brady. As the title indicates, the book is a versification of the Psalms for use as hymns; it was first published in 1696, and was the standard Anglican hymnal from that date until well into the nineteenth century.

Hardy clearly knew "The New Version" well. Mrs. Hardy tells us that as a child "Thomas was kept strictly at church on Sundays as usual, till he knew the Morning and Evening Services by heart including the rubrics, as well as large portions of the New Version of the Psalms" (*Early Life,* p. 23). To the end of his life he preferred Tate and Brady to all others; he wrote in his notebook in 1919 that he considered Watt's famous version of the Fortieth Psalm, "O God our help in ages past," inferior to Tate and Brady's

THE SEARCH FOR A FORM 87

version, "which contains some good and concise verse" (*Later Years,* p. 197), and he quoted parallel stanzas from the two versions to support his judgment. He disliked seeing changes made in the psalms, and complained that the new hymnal, *Hymns Ancient and Modern,* omitted "the most poetical verse" from the Thirty-fourth Psalm, which he had sung as a child in Tate and Brady's version. "Psalm the Hundred-and-Ninth," which Michael Henchard forces the choir to sing in *The Mayor of Casterbridge,* is from Tate and Brady; and there are also references to the New Version in the poems. "The liturgy of the Church of England is a noble thing," Hardy once remarked. "So are Tate and Brady's Psalms. These are the things that people need and should have."[40]

The metrics of "The New Version" are generally traditional—the common and long measures are the most frequent—but there are a few forms that are unusual. Two, in particular, seem to have appealed to Hardy. Psalm 148 is written in stanzas of eight lines, four three-stressed lines followed by four two-stressed lines, rhyming ababcddc. Hardy has a number of poems in stanzas which resemble this one: "A Spot," " 'I Have Lived with Shades,' " "Bereft," and "At Waking." (All are from early volumes, and one might infer that the influence of Tate and Brady on Hardy declined as he grew older and away from the church.) Psalm 149 is in stanzas of eight two-stressed lines, regularly made of an iamb followed by an anapest. Hardy employed this stanza frequently in his short-line poems. Other meters which Hardy used may also be found in Tate and Brady, but they are not unusual, and Hardy may have found them in any number of places.

The conclusion to be drawn from these observations on Hardy's metric is a fairly obvious one; Hardy did, as Gosse remarked, use a great many verse forms, but this abundance was not a sign of a rich, fruitful technical imagination. Rather, it was a sign of a fundamental disability in Hardy: he could not create a form which would transfer its excellences from one poem to another. While Hardy had, almost from the beginning, his own style, he never developed a characteristic form (in the sense that we might say that the dramatic monologue in blank verse was Browning's form). Of the best of Hardy's poems, scarcely two are in the same metrical form; Hardy went on to the end of his life trying again.

Part of this failure to find himself metrically was no doubt the result of his education, which was erratic and incomplete, and left him technically naïve and a little timid. He was prone to discover and assert with great enthusiasm what other people had known all their lives, and to theorize truisms at length. But the failure was surely due more to the disintegration of tradition which took place during his life, a process which he felt acutely as an Englishman and as a poet. Like other poets of his time, Hardy was left without a poetic vehicle adequate to his needs. He spent his life trying to build another out of old parts, and his *Collected Poems* is a scrapyard of ideas that did not work. That it also contains some great, living poems is testimony to the power of his peculiar poetic gifts to transcend what seem impossible obstacles, and to make poetry out of the ill-assorted materials that were all he had.

6

The Uses of Diction

POETIC DICTION presents a new problem to each poetic generation; every age has its own voice, and even the old ideas must be expressed in new words—the *mots* of one generation are the clichés of the next. This change in poetic language from one generation to another will be greater or less, depending on the continuity of values between them; the beliefs that can be salvaged will carry their own language with them. Where the break is violent, as it was between the High Victorians and their successors, the verbal changes will be correspondingly great. The change in language is never in itself a cause—Wordsworth did not adopt "language really used by men" because he fancied it but because he needed it; in the same way, Hardy's diction at its oddest is the product not of whim nor of incompetence but of necessity.

Yeats wrote of William Morris that "instead of the language of Chaucer and Shakespeare, its warp fresh from field and market—if the woof were learned—his age offered him a speech, exhausted from abstraction, that only returned to its full vitality when written learnedly and slowly."[41] Whether or not the exhaustion of English speech was actual, the best poets at the end of the last century felt it as such, and felt a compulsion to revitalize it. In the poetry of Hopkins, of Bridges, of Meredith, and of Yeats himself one finds a broadening of the sources of diction, and in some cases the creation of a new poetic diction of a highly individual kind.

The process has been carried further in the twentieth century, and for at least some of our contemporaries poetic diction is simply the full resources of the language (and sometimes of other languages as well, as when Pound uses Chinese ideograms). But the beginnings of the process are in the poetry of the late nineteenth century, and Hardy is more typical of the general development of modern poetic diction than is usually recognized. One might argue that the mixture of levels of diction in Hardy's verse is a Wessex version of the Pound-Eliot polyglot, and that it has its roots in the same cultural fact—the break-up of tradition. The difference is that for Hardy the tradition involved is that represented by English rustic life, and by folk-lore, and that his language therefore remains English, though not standard English, while for Pound and Eliot the break-up is in the culture of Western Europe, and hence their language is multi-lingual.

Like his contemporaries, Hardy set about to find a poetic diction adequate to his personal needs. He drew, as others did, upon the broad sources of language: the idioms of common speech; the vocabulary of special groups—architectural terms, for example; archaisms; old words in new or rare senses; regionalisms; and coined words and compounds. The results in Hardy's case were various and odd—poems which often seem to have been written "learnedly and slowly" indeed and, as Maugham said, with a blunt pencil. But if they are odd, they are also highly individual;

at best they have the vitality and strength of a fully realized personal vision. Sometimes that strength is very great, and it is in large part the product of the diction.

Hardy's diction was criticized from the first. Henry James deplored "the abomination of the language" in *Tess*,[42] and Patmore complained of *The Woodlanders*: "Why such a master of language should, in his latest work, have repeatedly indulged in such hateful modern slang as 'emotional' and 'phenomenal' (in the sense of 'extraordinary' instead of 'apparent') and in the equally detestable lingo of the drawing-room 'scientist' seems quite inexplicable."[43] And when the first part of *The Dynasts* appeared in 1904, the *Times Literary Supplement* remarked: "No one was ever, apparently, more insensible to the natural magic, the delight of purely poetic language."[44]

F. R. Leavis summarized the present critical attitude toward Hardy's diction:

If one says that he seems to have no sensitiveness for words, one recognizes at the same time that he has made a style out of stylelessness. There is something extremely personal about the gauche unshrinking mismarriages—group-mismarriages—of his diction, in which, with naïf aplomb, he takes as they come the romantic-poetical, the prosaic banal, the stilted literary, the colloquial, the archaistic, the erudite, the technical, the dialect word, the brand-new Hardy coinage.[45]

It is hard to object to the specifications of Leavis' charge: certainly plenty of examples of the varieties of diction which he lists can be found, if not on every page of the poems, at least liberally scattered through every volume. Elizabeth Hickson, in her study of Hardy's versification, identified the following oddities in the *Collected Poems*: 136 dialect words, 49 archaic, 145 obsolete, 51 rare, 36 poetic, 234 coined, 237 alliterative compounds.⁴⁶ A *Times Literary Supplement* article on the diction of *The Dynasts* adds twenty-one words used in senses not given in the *NED* and six words resurrected or re-invented, none of which has usages recorded in the *NED* later than the seventeenth century; one, "inkled," was apparently not used in print after 1370 until Hardy dug it up.⁴⁷

These varieties of diction, as Leavis points out, are likely to appear together in odd combinations, in "mismarriages" of the poetic with the prosaic, the dialectal with the coined, the archaistic with the colloquial, as in these lines:

> Still chew
> The kine, and moo
> In the meadows we used to wander through . . . .
>
> (*Collected Poems*, p. 496)

We can never be sure that a poem which begins on one level of diction will not shift to another—upward from prosaic to "stilted literary" ("Midnight on the Great Western" offers a good example of this kind of shift), or suddenly downward, from the "poetic" or "literary" to the colloquial or "prosaic banal." In certain circumstances such a shift may have poetic value—frequently in Hardy's poems it makes an ironic point; but in many instances the varieties of diction simply clash.

Occasionally it is apparent that the necessities of meter and rhyme have forced a "mismarriage" in a poem which is otherwise consistent in style. In "The Master and the Leaves" the single archaism, *treen*, is pretty clearly there to rhyme with *green* and *unseen*, rather than for any higher aesthetic reason. But not many of the mismarriages can be explained simply in terms of technical necessity; most of them must be regarded, like many of Hardy's inversions and other syntactical oddities, as freely chosen. But to infer from this, as Leavis does, that Hardy "seems to have no sensitiveness for words" is to oversimplify the case. It is more accurate, I think, to say (as I have said before) that Hardy did not have a conventional sense of poetic decorum.

William Archer got at this essential quality of Hardy's diction when he wrote that Hardy seemed "to lose all sense of local and historical perspective in language, seeing all the words in the dictionary on one plane, so to speak, and regarding them all as equally available and appropriate for any and every literary purpose."[48] The assumption that all language is, for poetic purposes, equally available is an invitation to disaster, and Hardy wrote a good many disastrous poems. But it does not necessarily imply insensitiveness to the words themselves; the insensitiveness is rather to certain conventional interrelationships *among* words. Such insensitiveness made Hardy susceptible to the awkward combinations of words that Leavis laments; but decorum may also be a restricting force, and Hardy's anarchic attitude toward language freed him for patterns of diction which are odd but often successful.

To make Leavis' evaluation of Hardy's diction entirely just, one must add certain qualifying remarks. Overawareness of the extremes of diction in Hardy may blind us to the large middle ground of poems which do not deviate noticeably from standard English. The ballads and ballad-like narratives, for example, approach the conversational idiom of the kind of people who might tell them—Hardy's Wessex countrymen—but deviate less from standard English. In them Hardy uses dialect and archaisms very sparingly: there is no non-standard English in "A Sunday Morning Tragedy," for example, and only one word—the obsolete *landskip*—in "A Trampwoman's Tragedy."

Apart from the ballads there are many other fine "standard-English" poems to be found in Hardy. Many of the best meditative poems exhibit a controlled use of language which is in itself simple and standard, and which derives its Hardyesque qualities from tone and syntax rather than from verbal oddities. This is a stanza from "Last Words to a Dumb Friend":

> Strange it is this speechless thing,
> Subject to our mastering,
> Subject for his life and food
> To our gift, and time, and mood;
> Timid pensioner of us Powers,
> His existence ruled by ours,
> Should—by crossing at a breath
> Into safe and shielded death,
> By the merely taking hence
> Of his insignificance—
> Loom as largened to the sense,
> Shape as part, above man's will,
> Of the Imperturbable.
>
> (*Collected Poems*, p. 622)

"Largened" and "the Imperturbable" are Hardyisms; but the rest of the stanza is plain language used with precision and subtlety; note the way in which the occasional long polysyllables are set off against a monosyllabic background, and the unifying effect of the recurrent language of government (subject, pensioner, Powers, ruled). The odd word or two may serve, as I have suggested before, to emphasize the *difference* of poetry, but the general effect is of direct speech.

Even where Hardy seems most uniquely himself, the effect may be achieved without recourse to non-standard English. There are, for example, certain favorite words, usually rather ordinary ones, which appear again and again in the poems. They fall into groups which can be related to aspects of Hardy's vision of things, and indeed one might, if given the vision, predict most of them. Hardy's steady pessimism is manifested in certain words which determine tone: *pale, sad, bleak, gloom, dim* are all common in the poems. Hardy's indifferent universe appears in words connoting vastness and emptiness: *vast, measureless, infinite, firmament, profound* (as a noun), *blankness*—and one might add *terrestrial* and *terrene,* which imply a cosmic view of the earth. Mechanism provides *mechanic, mindless, diurnal, rote,* and *pulse* and *mumming,* which have for Hardy connotations of unconscious mechanistic action. And finally, Hardy's preoccupation with mortality, mutability, and time appears in language of the supernatural: *phantom, ghost, spirit, spectral, wraith.*

Favorite words are not necessarily either good or bad; they are a part of every poet's equipment, and represent the individual qualities of his mind as well as imagery or themes do. But they may, through usage, lose their distinct significances and become simply counters, assertions of a relevance and meaning which does not actually exist.

Of Hardy's favorite words, *phantom* is the most frequently used—it occurs more than thirty times in the *Collected Poems* alone. It most commonly means an actual spirit from the dead, often a character in a dramatized incident, who speaks and is accepted by the human speaker as real:

>That a phantom should stalk there
>With me seemed nothing strange, and talk there . . . .

But it also carries other meanings in various poems: it may imply impermanence ("fleeting phantom-thought") or unreality ("whether a phantom . . . or was it some wrecked heart indeed"); it may mean imagination ("'tis but her phantom/Borne within my brain") or memory ("I do but the phantom retain/Of the maiden of yore"). (*Collected Poems,* pp. 562, 12, 342, 210, 55).

Most of these examples carry meanings of *phantom* which a dictionary will support—unreality, imagination, impermanence—but they frequently carry a secondary, contradictory meaning as well, since the phantom may be either real or unreal, a ghost or an illusion or a memory. The nature of the phantom is not often the crux of the matter (as it is for Hamlet and Macbeth); more often it is left in doubt simply because for Hardy the favorite word has lost its sharp distinctions of meaning, and has become simply a word for a vague emotion. In "The Lament of the Looking-Glass" the glass says:

> "I flash back phantoms of the night
>   That sometimes flit by me,
> I echo roses red and white—
>   The loveliest blooms that be—
> But now I never hold to sight
>   So sweet a flower as she."

(*Collected Poems,* p. 638)

The significance of *phantoms* in this stanza is at best imprecise. It stands in a catalogue of corporeal things which are not worth reflecting now that "she" is dead; but in this catalogue *phantoms* has no necessary role—its presence suggests an automatic response to a need for something mysterious, rather than conscious selection.

THE USES OF DICTION 97

One may speculate that *phantom* became a favorite of Hardy's through his fondness for the trope of the ghostly visitant, and that this trope is determined, in turn, by his inability to deal adequately with certain aspects of experience —in this case with the reality of evil. As a mechanist, Hardy logically should have denied that evil existed. But he was not logical; the poems and novels show that he felt that it *did* exist, and, moreover, its existence seems the one indubitable fact in the world as he saw it. He could not ascribe evil to human fallibility, as the religious-minded would, since for him man was a mummer, a victim. So he fell back, as he so often did, on his folk beliefs, on superstition—he made evil external but omnipresent, brought it in as ghosts and goblins and shadowy shapes, undefined because inexplicable, but always there. "Half my time," he wrote, "(particularly when I write verse) I believe—in the modern use of the word—not only in the things that Bergson does but in spectres, mysterious voices, intuitions, omens, dreams, haunted places, etc., etc." (*Later Years,* p. 271).

Hardy was incapable of creating human evil; the characters in the novels who are *really* evil are, in Hardy's phrase, "Mephistophelian visitants," not men. In the poems similar visitants appear, but less as incarnations of evil than simply as reminders that there do exist, even in this mindless, mechanistic universe, mysterious forces that work to our harm. Sometimes the trope of the visitant works to powerful and chilling effect—the lurking horror of "The Interloper" is a good example—but one can't help feeling that in time Hardy came to attach the responses appropriate to the trope to almost any terms denoting the supernatural, and to count on the simple repetition of those terms calling up the right responses: he made of the words a private ritual.

Pale offers a more extreme example of Hardy's failure to maintain an entirely responsible attitude toward language. Pallor is an attribute of virtually all of Hardy's lovers and ghosts; but the poems also include "to-day's pale pinions" (meaning apparently the wings of time); "A pale late plant of your once strong stock" (meaning Hardy); "a pale-winged token" (a moth); "the pale Form" (madness); "a pale past picture" (a dead man); "palest of sheet lightning"; and "pale phantasmal things" (a poet's fancies). (*Collected Poems*, 111, 253, 370, 459, 202, 309, 355). It is difficult to specify the quality which *pale* adds to these phrases, for the quality is often not related to the individual noun which the adjective modifies, but to Hardy's view of life, which cast an indiscriminate pallor over the things he saw. By calling a thing pale he assigned an emotion to it, and we must simply accept the assertion that the emotion is really there if we are to respond adequately to the poem.

A reader familiar with the poems will have no trouble extending this kind of analysis to the other favorite words I have mentioned. Most of them share, in some usages at least, the quality of assigned responses in excess of the situation—the quality of ritualized language.

There are certain other words in Hardy's poems which have no apparent relation to his thought, but which constitute an important aspect of his diction: such words as *rare, sweet,* and *bright,* which seem, like some of the "romantic-poetical" diction, to indicate a failure of vision, a momentary inability to realize a situation. There are many rare maidens in Hardy; the same epithet is also applied to cider-makings, a man's path among men, and Life. The term usually combines the common meanings of scarcity and excellence; sometimes, however, it seems simply to indicate something vaguely desirable and, because Hardy's desires were generally retrospective, something located in the past. In a statement like

> This Life runs dry
> That once ran rare

no specific meaning is possible; one cannot relate *rare* either to its verb or to its apparent antonym *dry*. The word, like other favorite words, must be taken on faith, as meaning what Hardy says it means. The same might be said of *sweet, bright, true* (usually in the phrase "so true"), and other such substitutes for precise language.

In an examination of Hardy's diction the favorite words are important. They constitute the most distinctive single element in the diction of the poems. We cannot, however, overlook the collective aspect of diction, the interrelationships which exist among different kinds of language operating within a single context. Leavis calls these interrelationships in Hardy's poetry "mismarriages," and implies that they are simply unfortunate accidents. It seems to me wiser, in view of the evidence, to assume that Hardy knew what he was doing, even when most naïf and gauche, and that his juxtapositions of oddly-matched words might be, at least in intention, mismarriages of convenience, a device for establishing tensions on the level of diction. Such an assumption does not deny the failures, which are obvious; but it does make it possible to look for poetic purposes in the language, and perhaps to reach a greater understanding of how the poems work than would otherwise be possible.

At any rate, Hardy *thought* he knew what he was doing —he was drawing upon the full potential of the English language. In a conversation with Archer, he said:

I have no sympathy with the criticism which would treat English as a dead language—a thing crystallised at an arbitrarily selected stage of its existence, and bidden to forget that it has a past and deny that it has a future. Purism, whether in grammar or vocabulary, almost always means ignorance. Language was made before grammar, not grammar before language. And as for the people who make it their business to insist on the utmost possible impoverishment of our English vocabulary, they seem to me to ignore the lessons of history, science, and common sense.[49]

Hardy was certainly no purist. And yet, one cannot read the *Collected Poems* without becoming aware that there are wide variations in diction from poem to poem, that all poems do not contain all varieties of diction, and that there seems to be a correlation between kinds of diction and kinds of poems; Hardy does seem to have made distinctions, though not in any conventional manner.

A notebook entry of 1900 contains this diagram and note:

	VERSE		
FANCIFUL	MEDITATIVE	SENTIMENTAL	PASSIONATE
	LANGUAGE OF COMMON SPEECH		
POETIC DICTION			

The confusion of thought to be observed in Wordsworth's teaching in his essay in the Appendix to *Lyrical Ballads* seems to arise chiefly out of his use of the word 'imagination'. He should have put the matter somewhat like this: In works of *passion and sentiment* (not 'imagination and sentiment') the language of verse is the language of prose. In works of *fancy* (or imagination) 'poetic diction' (of the real kind) is proper, and even necessary. The diagram illustrates my meaning (*Later Years*, p. 85).

The diagram is comical if taken as a system—one does not write poetry from a chart on the wall. But it is valuable to us if we regard it as a statement of inclinations in method which must, after all, be largely intuitive in a poet.

Although the terminology of the diagram is rather vague, its meaning in relation to Hardy's poems seems to be roughly this: *Passionate,* the ballads and narratives of ballad-like incidents; *Sentimental,* the poems of recollection, especially of love and lovers, like "To Lizbie Brown" and "Days to Recollect" and some of the 1912-13 poems; *Meditative,* the introspective, first-person monologues—"Looking Across," "In Tenebris," "Quid Hic Agis?"; *Fanciful,* the philosophical dialogues with God, the Mother, and such Powers, perhaps the conversations with ghosts, and the conventional love lyrics like "Come Not; Yet Come."

Along the scale in the diagram one can arrange the varieties of diction which Hardy uses: the erudite, the technical, the stilted literary, the romantic-poetical are all "poetic diction," and occur in fanciful, meditative, and occasionally in sentimental poems, but rarely in the passionate (i.e., ballads and narratives); the colloquial, the archaistic, and the prosaic banal provide the "language of common speech," and occur in the poems much as the diagram indicates. The coinages seem to be scattered rather indiscriminately through the poems, though there are more of them in the fanciful and meditative poems and fewer in the ballads. Apparently, then, Hardy did have his own sense of decorum—for certain kinds of poetic expression, certain kinds of language were appropriate.

Hardy's comment on his diagram makes another point worth lingering over: he refers to "the real kind" of poetic diction, implying that he was aware that there is also a false kind. When he found "poetic" rhetorical devices which seemed to him "the real kind," as he did in Barnes's otherwise rustic poems, he defended them as "justified by the art of every age when they can claim to be . . . singularly precise and beautiful definitions of what is signified." (The examples he cites are "the blue-hill'd worold," "the wide-horn'd cow," and "the grey-topp'd heights of Paladore," Preface to *Barnes*, p. xi). He also had firm ideas about the false kind; when Robert Graves visited him at Max Gate, Hardy counselled the younger poet to remove from a poem the phrase "the scent of thyme," because it was "one of the *clichés* which poets of his generation studied to avoid."[50] Between "the wide-horn'd cow" and "the scent of thyme" there may not seem much to choose. But there is this difference, that one phrase is an effort at direct description of the phenomenal world, while the other depends on conventional poetic associations.

Examples of extended use of poetic diction, in his own sense of the phrase, are fairly rare in Hardy, though there are some. A glance at one of the best examples may be useful in indicating the nature of Hardy's poetic diction and the way it works in a poem; the example is " 'According to the Mighty Working' ":

I

When moiling seems at cease
   In the vague void of night-time,
   And heaven's wide roomage stormless
   Between the dusk and light-time,
   And fear at last is formless,
We call the allurement Peace.

II

Peace, this hid riot, Change,
This revel of quick-cured mumming,
This never truly being,
This evermore becoming,
This spinner's wheel onfleeing
Outside perception's range.

(*Collected Poems*, p. 541)

One is immediately conscious of certain favorite Hardy effects: vastness in "wide roomage stormless"; determinism in "mumming" and the "spinner's wheel"; semi-darkness; a turmoil of verbals. The language is abstract—one is conscious of words-as-words rather than as images (especially in *Peace, Change, being,* and *becoming,* but pretty consistently throughout the poem)—but it is not heavy; there are none of the ponderous Latinized polysyllables that burden the bad poems in this vein, and in fact monosyllables predominate. Certain words and constructions will sound familiar to any reader of Hardy's poems—*roomage, light-time,* and *onfleeing* are typical of Hardy's most common coinages, combinations of plain words and plain prefixes, just odd enough to force a pause, but unexceptionable. The inversion, "wide roomage stormless," is also characteristic, as is the use of feminine rhyme. There is also a complicated sound pattern which gives each stanza its own unity and lends the poem the textural interest which it does not get from imagery (the images seem intentionally suppressed to emphasize the verbal, words-as-words effect).

Although the language is unusual, not much of it could be called "poetic diction" in the conventional sense of the phrase: Hardy has mixed his varieties of diction freely, but on the whole unobtrusively and successfully. The impression the poem gives is not one of straining toward eccentricity, but of language used to its full potential, yet with ease and control. The verse form, with its short lines, regular meter, and framing rhymes (*cease-Peace, Change-range*) contributes considerably to this effect.

Sometimes, of course, Hardy's control of his diction was faulty; sometimes his "poetic" language entangled him and produced lines like

> "Ha," they hollowly hackered,
> "You come, forsooth. . . ."
>
> (*Collected Poems*, p. 363)

and

> The moon was at the window-square,
> Deedily brooding in deformed decay. . . .
>
> (*Collected Poems*, p. 484)

But generally he had the sense to use his oddities sparingly and for particular reasons. The effectiveness of much good poetry lies in the unexpected word; in Hardy's verse this word is usually from a level of diction other than that dominant in the poem: an archaism, regionalism, coinage or "poetical" term in a colloquial context, as for example in the last stanza of "In Time of 'The Breaking of Nations'":

> Yonder a maid and her wight
> Come whispering by:
> War's annals will fade into night
> Ere their story die.
>
> (*Collected Poems*, p. 511)

The diction of this poem as a whole is extremely plain. In the last stanza the poetic words *wight* and *Ere* are therefore noticeable, and serve to shift the tone upward and out of time, from the solemn description of human and natural endurance to the assertion of the immortality of love.

This device—the juxtaposition of varieties of diction in a single poem—is Hardy's most characteristic verbal mannerism; it is as apparent in his best poems as in his most dismal failures. The effect, when the poem succeeds, is ironic; for the kind of diction one uses implies an attitude toward the subject, and the juxtaposition of diverse attitudes to a single state or event produces irony. The mixing of diction is, then, another form of the antinomial pattern which is the controlling structural principle of Hardy's art.

Irony may also operate in the relation between the language of a poem and the situation which it presents. One of Hardy's finest poems, " 'And There Was a Great Calm' " (*Collected Poems*, p. 557), works in this way. One could almost chart the course of the diction in the poem graphically—from abstraction to particularity to abstraction, or from "poetic" and "literary" to colloquial and back again. The poem starts on a level of high (even capitalized) abstraction, representing a single, unqualified attitude toward the event—War.

> There had been years of Passion—scorching, cold,
> And much Despair, and Anger heaving high,
> Care whitely watching, Sorrows manifold,
> Among the young, among the weak and old,
> And the pensive Spirit of Pity whispered, "Why?"

Against this abstract attitude of compassion Hardy sets the realities of war: the line in the second stanza, "And 'Hell!' and 'Shell!' were yapped at Lovingkindness," sets up the opposition between the fact and the emotion.

In the third stanza, the approach to the reality begins with the plain language of war, first experienced *as words*:

> The feeble folk at home had grown full-used
> To "dug-outs," "snipers," "Hun," from the war-adept
> In the mornings heard, and at evetides perused;
> To day-dreamt men in millions, when they mused—
> To nightmare-men in millions when they slept.

"The feeble folk" are set against the "war adept," and the opposition is extended in a typical Hardyesque antinomy—"day-dreamt men" against "nightmare-men."

The fourth and fifth stanzas move toward the war, though they retain some distance through poetic language and syntax—the point of view is still that of the outside observer, who asks, with "the bereft, and meek, and lowly":

> Will men some day be given to grace? yea, wholly,
> And in good sooth, as our dreams used to run?"

The center of the poem is in the sixth stanza, "out there," that is, at the physical center of the situation, on the battlefield. The language in this stanza alone is entirely plain, the reaction of the fighting men to the end of the war, a reaction devoid of emotional language, or abstractions, or compassion. The language is moving because of its plainness, made more striking in the frame of "poetic" language and abstractions formed by preceding and following stanzas.

> Breathless they paused. Out there men raised their glance
> To where had stood those poplars lank and lopped,
> As they had raised it through the four years' dance
> Of Death in the now familiar flats of France;
> And murmured, "Strange, this! How? All firing stopped?"

From this center the level of diction gradually rises, through abstractions ("Rage and Wrong") and locutions like "Waft-winged engines" (meaning airplanes) to the question which the Spirit of Pity had asked in stanza one: "Why?" But where the question when first asked expressed simple compassion, "why war?" it appears in the last line as a final cosmic irony—"why peace?" The "Sinister Spirit" sees the whole pattern of war and the termination of war as necessary: "It had to be!" but the Spirit of Pity, which Hardy says elsewhere represents "the Universal Sympathy of human nature," can find reason in neither event, and its question remains unanswerable, as Hardy found it.

The range of diction and the delicacy with which it is controlled in the poem is remarkable, and accounts for the poem's peculiar power. Hardy was never afraid of abstractions or of personifications—he used them freely, and, one may feel, with a naïve assurance which was not always well-founded. In this instance, however, the contrast of an abstract attitude (in itself a completely *right* moral position, a sort of agonized compassion), and the event, which stripped of all but the plainest descriptive language is yet more moving because more real, is brilliantly effective; the poem is a *tour de force* in the Hardy style.

" 'And There Was a Great Calm' " is fundamental Hardy —a poem articulating the unresolved opposition of *is* and *should be,* man's failure to find in experience an order which would make that experience tolerable. (It is not surprising that Hardy responded so deeply and so finely to war; war offered him a supreme dramatic example of the meaningless destruction which he found throughout existence.) Hardy's use of language in the poem, like his other poetic mannerisms here and elsewhere, stems from his philosophical failure to resolve conflicts and contradictions. I said of his style in general that it does not operate within a coherent system because his universe doesn't. The same may be said of his diction—it is the language of lost order. In this it is both very personal and very modern. For Hardy there could be no *a priori* limits set upon the kinds of language available to him; only the necessities of the event dictated the language in which it was recorded. Every poem was a new start, another desperate assault on chaos; his weapons were all the words he had. The results, on the level of language as on the level of belief, were tensions, conflicts, antinomies—but no conclusions, no resolutions.

For the expression of Hardy's vision of existence, such odd personal habits of diction were inevitable and right. Hardy himself felt them to be so. Robert Graves recalled that Hardy, late in life, regretted that he had listened to professional critics, for "on their advice he had cut out dialect-words from his early poems, though they had no exact synonyms to fit the context. And still the critics were plaguing him. One of them recently complained of a poem of his where he had written 'his shape smalled in the distance.' Now what in the world else could he have written?"[51] And this is perhaps the final word on Hardy's diction. In the world he saw, what else could he have written?

7

The Two Worlds of Imagery

WHEN WE SPEAK of a poet's "vision" we are using a veiled metaphor which expresses a basic truth about the poetic process—that in his art the poet makes his sense of reality actual by embodying it in the visible things of this world, that is, in images. Images are the forms of ideas and feelings, the intimate gestures by which the creative mind reveals itself.

Certainly Hardy thought of art in this way. He was aware that representational accuracy was not enough, and for this reason preferred, among landscape painters, Turner —"the mad, late Turner." Of Turner's water colors he wrote:

each is a landscape *plus* a man's soul .... He first recognizes the impossibility of really reproducing on canvas all that is in a landscape; then gives for that which cannot be reproduced a something else which shall have upon the spectator an approximative effect to that of the real. He said, in his maddest and greatest days: "What pictorial drug can I dose a man with, which shall affect his eyes somewhat in the manner of this reality which I cannot carry to him?" (*Early Life,* p. 283).

Here Hardy makes two important points: first, that art is a complex of objective reality and subjective response (landscape *plus* a man's soul); and second, that the artist, if he is to communicate this complex, must select his details for their effect and not for their fidelity to the objective fact (a formulation which is close to Eliot's "objective correlative"). Hardy saw art as a process of selection,

a disproportioning—(*i.e.*, distorting, throwing out of proportion) —of realities, to show more clearly the features that matter in those realities, which, if merely copied or reported inventorially, might possibly be observed, but would more probably be overlooked (*Early Life*, p. 299).

He praised Crabbe for "a novel, good, microscopic touch" in his poetry; "He gives," Hardy wrote, "surface without outline, describing his church by telling *the colour of the lichens*" (*Later Years*, p. 57). We recognize at once how much of this—the "good, microscopic touch," "the features that matter"—describes Hardy's own practice; like most poet-critics he found in the art of others what he sought in his own.

The "features that matter" in Hardy's poems can be sorted into a few antinomial patterns corresponding to the "philosophy" which we have already discussed. There are virtually no images which do not fit into these patterns; the sum of the imagery is Hardy's view of the world, and the limitations are the limitations of that view. This is so literally true that without the didactic poems and other philosophical remarks one could infer the whole pattern of Hardy's thought simply from his image-picture of the world.

Actually, for Hardy there are, as we might by now expect, *two* worlds, and these two form the fundamental opposition which determines the image-structure of his poems. One is the world of light—of day and sun and spring, of flowers and bright colors, of youth and life. The other world is dark—its images are dusk and night, winter, rain and snow, age, and death. The two worlds act upon each other in the antinomial manner that I have already described as central to Hardy's metrics and diction.

Of the two worlds, the latter figures far more prominently in the poems, and is the main theme against which the other forms a counterpoint. It is the world of Hardy's mature vision, stripped of illusion, pessimistic, "neutral-tinted." Hardy offers his most elaborate defense of this literary grayness in the first chapter of his grayest novel, *The Return of the Native*:

Fair prospects wed happily with fair times; but alas, if times be not fair! Men have oftener suffered from the mockery of a place too smiling for their reason than from the oppression of surroundings oversadly tinged. Haggard Egdon appealed to a subtler and scarcer instinct, to a more recently learnt emotion, than that which responds to the sort of beauty called charming and fair.

Indeed, it is a question if the exclusive reign of this orthodox beauty is not approaching its last quarter. The new Vale of Tempe may be a gaunt waste in Thule: human souls may find themselves in closer and closer harmony with external things wearing a sombreness distasteful to our race when it was young. The time seems near, if it has not actually arrived, when the chastened sublimity of a moor, a sea, or a mountain will be all of nature that is absolutely in keeping with the moods of the more thinking among mankind (pp. 4-5).

This is Hardy's inverted evolution again: man, as he has developed the capacity for thought, has evolved away from his place in the natural scheme of things, and as his consciousness has grown, his sense of alienation has grown, too. Hence, for "the more thinking of mankind," the idea of natural beauty must change to fit the new melancholy. The world that Hardy chose to picture, then, was an image of his own philosophy, a metaphor for the modern condition, as he saw it.

In his notebook for 1887, Hardy wrote:

I feel that Nature is played out as a Beauty, but not as a Mystery. I don't want to see landscapes, *i.e.*, scenic paintings of them, because I don't want to see the original realities—as optical effects, that is. I want to see the deeper reality underlying the scenic, the expression of what are sometimes called abstract imaginings (*Early Life*, p. 242).

This seems an odd remark, coming from the Bard of Wessex. But it is quite accurate to say that as a poet Hardy was not much interested in the scenic as such. There are no literal landscapes in Hardy's poems, and Wessex rarely figures as the specific scene of an action. The poems are true pictures, but only in the sense that they offer images of a "deeper reality"; of a world gray with despair, deprived of every faith except the grim expectations of evolution; a world in which man is helpless and uncomforted, and life is "a thing to be put up with"; and in which Nature is played out as a Beauty, because for man natural beauty is a bitter irony at his expense.

The most striking quality of Hardy's somber world is its colorlessness. The poems tend more to chiaroscuro than to color gradations. Hardy set the scene of "The Lacking Sense" in "a sad-coloured landscape," and this is essentially the locale of most of his poems. If there is any color, it is faded or fading—a sunset, or the coals in a grate, or wilted flowers—a transitory rather than a permanent part of reality.

This is also true of Hardy's use of light. He preferred the changing times of day—dawn and dusk—when colors are flattened toward a common grayness, and the earth is "neutral-tinted." The setting of "The Darkling Thrush" is characteristic:

> I leant upon a coppice gate
> When Frost was spectre-gray,
> And Winter's dregs made desolate
> The weakening eye of day.
> The tangled bine-stems scored the sky
> Like strings of broken lyres,
> And all mankind that haunted nigh
> Had sought their household fires.
>
> (*Collected Poems*, p. 137)

The pictorial effect is of silhouette, black against gray. Even the frost is "spectre-gray"; gray is by far Hardy's favorite color—it is, in fact, about as colorful as his dark world ever gets. Night, particularly midnight, also figures prominently in the poems, often to draw a white-black contrast between lighted interiors and the vast darkness outside, which is emptiness and mystery and ignorance and time—all the dark realities that man hides from beside his fire.

There are virtually no daylight, sunshine poems (some exceptions to this statement will be discussed later). When daylight does appear it is the gray light of overcast, bitter days. "In a Waiting-Room" is typical:

> On a morning sick as the day of doom
> With the drizzling gray
> Of an English May....
>
> (*Collected Poems*, p. 487)

Some of Hardy's most striking, individual images are in this mood:

>   . . . I
> Saw morning harden upon the wall. . .
>
> . . . the morning sky grew grayer
> And day crawled in.
>
> . . . the fainting light
> Succumbs to the crawl of night.
>
> (*Collected Poems,* pp. 318, 560, 708)

It is obvious from the verbs that Hardy's daylight does not perform the customary image-function of day—his dawns are not dawns of hope, and there is no peace in his dusk. Meredith's phrase, "his twilight view of life," is a quite literal description of the physical setting of the poems, as well as of the thought behind them.

The grayness of Hardy's light carries over into other aspects of his imagery. His seasons are autumn and winter —the gray, dead, twilight seasons. Out of these seasons come appropriate seasonal images—falling leaves, bare trees, gray skies: "It never looks like summer here," as one poem puts it. Weather imagery is a part of the seasons; wind, rain, fog, and snow—the weather of suffering—prevail. In one group of eight poems in *Human Shows* there occur three snow storms, a wind storm, rain, ice, and a heavy frost. The sun never shines.

Such details of the physical setting of the poems have in common the fact that they all can be related metaphorically to death (a subject for which Hardy seems to have had an abnormal concern). Hardy's necrophilia is nowhere more clear than in the use he makes of the imagery of setting: dawn is "the pale corpse-like birth/Of this diurnal unit"; rain-drops hang on the bramble "with the cold listless lustre of a dead man's eye"; clouds are "dead-white as a corpse outlaid"; winter is "the skeleton time"; dead leaves hang on the trees "like suspended criminals"; the trees are "skeleton-thin" (*Collected Poems,* pp. 105, 592, 208, 710, 673, 463). It is interesting to notice here that nature does not provide images of death; death, rather, provides images of nature—death is the "deeper reality."

In this dead world the focus is not ordinarily on the scene, but on the creatures in it, or more precisely on the possible meaning of their presence there. Nature itself is never the point of Hardy's poems; the point is man's efforts to find his place in a nature which is indifferent to him. Hardy wrote:

An object or mark raised or made by man on a scene is worth ten times any such formed by unconscious Nature. Hence clouds, mists and mountains are unimportant beside the wear on a threshold, or the print of a hand (*Early Life,* p. 153).

This taste for the man-made is obvious in the novels: the most imposing feature of Egdon Heath is Rainbarrow; the focal point of the country landscape in *Jude* is the spires of Christminster. It is also true of the poems that in them we look not at nature, but at man in nature. There is always the human element present.

There are occasionally other dumb creatures, as well—personal pets, fallow deer, a stray cat, wild and caged birds. The animals appear infrequently, but the birds are common. Their presence can be explained by their function as images. Birds are traditionally omens, and Hardy often uses them to give a sense of impending dread, as in "During Wind and Rain":

> Ah, no; the years, the years;
> See, the white storm-birds wing across!
>
> (*Collected Poems,* p. 465)

But more frequently birds are victims, victims both of human cruelty and of the blind cruelty of nature. They are, in various poems, starving or starved, blinded, caged, or shot by hunters, and by their sad fates they provide images of the inevitable harshness and suffering of existence. Hardy used the same device in *Tess*—the wounded birds that Tess finds in the woods and the "strange birds from behind the North Pole" that appear in the wintry turnip field suffer as Tess suffers, because "the President of the Immortals" will have it so.

From these observations on the nature of Hardy's dark world we might easily compose a typical Hardy scene. A heath: winter: the sky gray: freezing rain falling: foreground a leafless tree: beneath it a bird that has starved to death: a poet regards the bird. If this seems a crude burlesque, consider the following stage direction to "Winter in Durnover Field":

> SCENE.—*A wide stretch of fallow ground recently sown with wheat, and frozen to iron hardness. Three large birds walking about thereon, and wistfully eyeing the surface. Wind keen from north-east: sky a dull grey.*
>
> (*Collected Poems*, p. 136)

Any reader of Hardy will recall many equally bleak scenes in both the novels and the poems.

This composite picture of the Hardy-scene is in effect an image of one term, one pole of his philosophical pattern. It is a traditional view, and the individual images which express it are also, in the main, traditional. The relation of winter and death goes back to earliest myth; the similar use of darkness and night is as ancient; and for the emotional significance of bad weather we might consider any number of ballads, from "Sir Patrick Spens" to "The Ancient Mariner," as well as *Macbeth* and *King Lear*. I have discussed Hardy's debt to Shakespeare and the ballads before; I do not mean at this point to suggest that Hardy owed a direct debt to either for his imagery, but rather that a common view of man's fate—the tragic sense of life—runs through the myth makers, the ballad makers, and Shakespeare, to Hardy, and that it is imaged in the same terms.

The tragic archetypes appear, again, in certain books of the Old Testament, particularly in Psalms, Ecclesiastes, and Job—what we might call the tragic books. The direct influence of these books on Hardy is clear and demonstrable. In the novels there are many scenes built on Biblical parallels or extended references (the last chapter of *Jude,* for example), and quotations and allusions by the hundreds; in the poems there are numerous quotations and allusions, too. It is obvious that Hardy knew at least some portions of the Bible well, especially the darker books of the Old Testament, and that he read them frequently enough to have at his command a wealth of allusion and imagery.

A glance at the imagery of Job will show the similarity to Hardy's method and point of view. Job is composed of a recurrent pattern of simple, archetypal images, a surprisingly small number of them, considering the length of the book. The most common are images of light and dark, shadow and cloud. Chapter Three, from which Hardy borrowed the great curse for *Jude,* is virtually all light and dark imagery:

> Let the day perish wherein I was born, and the night in which it was said, There is a man child conceived.
>
> Let that day be darkness, let not God regard it from above, neither let the light shine upon it.

> Let darkness and the shadow of death stain it; let a cloud dwell upon it; let the blackness of the day terrify it.

As in Hardy, the relentless passing of time, imaged in fading daylight, seasonal change, and the harvesting of crops, is a constant reminder of man's mortality. And death is always there, in the worms and the dust, the fallen leaf and the dead flowers (all common images in Hardy's poems).

The weather, in Job, is consistently foul. There are winds and storms, rains, floods, lightning, and thunder. Job's God does not manifest Himself in light, but out of the whirlwind. The thirty-eighth chapter is all weather, and all of it bad; it is a turbulent image of the uncontrollable, hostile, baffling universe in which man finds himself. Hardy used the same images to the same ends.

A number of other images common to Hardy's poems and the Book of Job might be mentioned—stones and rocks, traps and snares, stars—but the point has, I think, been made. Tragic works of art repeat certain images which are eternally symbolic in the human mind, as the tragic sense is eternal; Hardy draws his most powerful and most characteristic imagery from this tragic tradition.

It is striking, in the light of the many Biblical echoes in his poetry, that Hardy made virtually no use of the many images and symbols in the Bible which are directly related to the Christian myth—that he did not, for example, draw substantially upon either Genesis or the Synoptic Gospels, and that when he did employ a specifically Christian image, as in "Near Lanivet, 1872," he felt compelled to explicate the gesture (of crucifixion) and so seriously weakened a potentially good poem. Writing and thinking as he did outside the Christian faith of his time, Hardy was denied the poetic advantages of that faith, the structural and imagistic values of the Christian myth; he could not, that is, make the assumptions about his Christian images that a Christian poet would make. The doctrines which he had embraced in place of his Christian faith were not such as had produced poetry or a body of poetic imagery—there was no poetry of any importance in the deterministic tradition. Hardy drew, therefore, no doubt instinctively, upon what Maud Bodkin calls the "psychological tradition," those archetypal images which run through mankind's great experiences from the beginnings, and which are unrelated to doctrine.

I have dwelt at length on Hardy's dark world because it is primary, a complex projection of his pessimism. But there is also the other world, the world of light, which, though it occurs less frequently and offers fewer images, is nevertheless important in the total picture as a qualifier of the darkness and of the pessimism as well, as one term, that is, in the antinomial pattern as it is manifested in imagery.

The details of this world, like those of the other, dark world, are traditional and archetypal, to be experienced at a level below consciousness. Essentially they form the antithesis of the primary Hardy scene, for this world is bright with light and color; the season is spring or summer, the time noon, the sky clear:

> My lover and I
> Walked under a sky
> Of blue with a leaf-wove awning of green,
> In the burn of August. . . .
>
> (*Collected Poems,* p. 316)

The scene is out of doors, and there is a gay delight in life and the world. This is, in short, the world of youth, when hope and joy are imaged in season, sunlight, and weather.

It does not, however, exist by itself—there is scarcely one pure "youth" poem in the whole of Hardy. Its function is rather to act in tension with the dark world, to emphasize that world by opposition at the same time that it qualifies through irony the otherwise too simple pessimism of the dark-world attitude. Its role is secondary and supporting; the light-world never provides the point of view. It is always in the past tense, a world seen from a distance, in the memory, and seen with the cold eyes of maturity. The contrast in which it functions is the old opposition of illusion and reality, and youth is the bright illusion.

The vision of youth is false because it is short-sighted, sees only the present, and ignores the fundamental truths of change and mortality. In terms of imagery, the absence of death images in the world of youth makes that world untrue. Its brightness, warmth, and color mask the dark, ultimate reality; the poet, from his somber vantage point of age and disillusionment, supplies that reality, as a dark frame to the bright picture, by seeing the moment as a transitory event in the stream of time. So, in "At Middle-field Gate in February," the speaker, looking on a rain-drenched, fog-wrapped winter day, recalls the same scene in summer sunlight (i.e., in youth):

> How dry it was on a far-back day
>   When straws hung the hedge and around,
> When amid the sheaves in amorous play
> In curtained bonnets and light array
>   Bloomed a bevy now underground.
>
> (*Collected Poems*, p. 451)

The last line is a judgment of youth's first fallacy; but the poem is saved from cynical sourness by the nostalgia which the speaker feels for that time which was happy, for all its ignorance of life. (We find the same theme in the later poems of Yeats; the two old men had much in common.)

Wisdom lies in the world of darkness, but it is expensive wisdom. The wise man—philosopher and ironic pessimist—acknowledges the fact and imagery of death, but there is small comfort in the knowledge and no real reconciliation to the fact.

> Wintertime nighs;
> But my bereavement Pain
> It cannot bring again:
> Twice no one dies. . . .
>
> Black is night's cope;
> But death will not appal
> One who, past doubtings all,
> Waits in unhope.

(*Collected Poems*, p. 153)

This, briefly, is all the meaning and justification that Hardy's world offers—the solace of disenchantment. The darkness is the philosophical state of Hardy's modern men, the Clym Yeobrights and Jude Fawleys, deprived of the reassuring light of belief, who must live honestly in darkness or delude themselves. The "In Tenebris" sequence develops this point at length; significantly, epigraphs to all three parts are from Psalms.

Let us examine an example of the way in which Hardy's two worlds co-exist within a poem. The poem is "During Wind and Rain," one of Hardy's finest lyrics:

They sing their dearest songs—
He, she, all of them—yea,
Treble and tenor and bass,
  And one to play;
With the candles mooning each face. . .
  Ah, no; the years O!
How the sick leaves reel down in throngs!

They clear the creeping moss—
Elders and juniors—aye,
Making the pathways neat,
  And the garden gay;
And they build a shady seat. . .
  Ah, no; the years, the years;
See, the white storm-birds wing across!

They are blithely breakfasting all—
Men and maidens—yea,
Under the summer tree,
  With a glimpse of the bay,
While pet fowl come to the knee . . .
  Ah, no; the years O!
And the rotten rose is ript from the wall.

They change to a high new house,
He, she, all of them—aye,
Clocks and carpets and chairs
  On the lawn all day,
And brightest things are theirs. . .
  Ah, no; the years, the years;
Down their carved names the rain-drop ploughs.

(*Collected Poems*, pp. 465-66)

The structural pattern of the poem is simple: in each stanza the first five lines provide an image of youth; the refrain intrudes mortality upon the scene; and the image of the last line asserts the inevitable victory of death. The peculiar fineness of the poem consists in the tenderness of the youth-images—there is great sympathy and pathos and regret in them, for youth is a lovely world, though its features fade—and in the fact that the poem speaks entirely through its imagery.

As one might expect, the scenes of youth are in sunlight or soft candlelight, in summer, in a garden "with a glimpse of the bay," and "brightest things" are theirs. The images are bright, vivid, pictorial. The terminal mortality images, on the other hand, are brief, and depend more on immediate emotional response than on pictorial realization. They are all familiar from the preceding discussion and, for that matter, from the great tragic voices that I have mentioned as being in Hardy's tradition: falling leaves, ominous birds, dead flowers, rain—these are the archetypes of death. In this poem, Hardy's two worlds are brilliantly set in tension, and brilliantly clear. The poem does not judge between the two, but simply demonstrates through juxtaposition how each term denies the other. No resolution is offered; in Hardy's view, no resolution is possible.

"During Wind and Rain" illustrates two points about Hardy's imagery—it is homogeneous and self-contained, and it is highly selective. Hardy's images, without notable exception, are native to the world which we call Wessex. This does not, of course, make the poems "Wessex poems" in the sense that Hardy's best novels are "Wessex novels"; that is, the poems neither create nor depend on a sense of locale. By selecting the "features that matter," Hardy keeps the focus of the poem on the emotional weighting rather than on the image itself.

Individual images are not often striking; they derive their effectiveness more from the accretions of emotion which tradition has given to certain experiences than from pictorial vividness or the impact of oddness. The scenes are rarely realized in any great detail, and few readers, I should think, actually visualize the rain and the darkness: archetypal imagery bypasses this step to comprehension. The emotion-producing detail is there—the falling leaf or the night wind—but the specific surroundings are largely ignored. The imagery produces tone rather than picture; it is, in the words of Turner that Hardy quotes: "something else which shall have upon the spectator an approximative effect to that of the real." Images may, on occasion, be sharp and clear—Hardy had an eye for the small, significant detail—but the background is seldom filled in, so that pictorially the images are incomplete, like a painter's rough cartoons. They are not, of course, any less effective for their bareness.

This imagistic bareness, this unwillingness to indulge the sensual for its own sake, is simply another aspect of the restraint and decorum which characterized Hardy's entire life. Mrs. Hardy tells us that he could not stand to be touched, and one senses this fastidious withdrawal from direct physical contact with life in much of the poetry. For example, he rarely used images involving the "contact" senses of touch and taste, or the kinesthetic sense, preferring images of sight and sound—the senses which can operate at a distance. Through such devices he made his poems those of an observer rather than of an agent; his speaker is consistently *outside* the event, observing it but not involved in it. "Afterwards," one of the most imagistic (and one of the loveliest) of Hardy's poems, demonstrates this point very well:

When the Present has latched its postern behind my tremulous stay,
And the May month flaps its glad green leaves like wings,
Delicate-filmed as new-spun silk, will the neighbours say,
"He was a man who used to notice such things"?

If it be in the dusk when, like an eyelid's soundless blink,
The dewfall-hawk comes crossing the shades to alight
Upon the wind-warped upland thorn, a gazer may think,
"To him this must have been a familiar sight."

If I pass during some nocturnal blackness, mothy and warm,
When the hedgehog travels furtively over the lawn,
One may say, "He strove that such innocent creatures should come to no harm,
But he could do little for them; and now he is gone."

If, when hearing that I have been stilled at last, they stand at the door,
Watching the full-starred heavens that winter sees,
Will this thought rise on those who will meet my face no more,
"He was one who had an eye for such mysteries"?

And will any say when my bell of quittance is heard in the gloom,
And a crossing breeze cuts a pause in its outrollings,
Till they rise again, as they were a new bell's boom,
"He hears it not now, but used to notice such things"?

(*Collected Poems*, p. 521)

The speaker in this poem is very like Hardy as I have been describing him—a man who "notices" from a distance, who has "an eye for much mysteries," who is familiar with the sights and sounds of his rural world. The principal images in the poem are, very characteristically, observed from a distance: the hawk on the thorn, the hedgehog on the lawn, the stars, the distant bell. Of these the speaker is a sensitive and precise observer; he knows the texture of new leaves and the way hawks and hedgehogs move. But though he "notices such things," he can do little for them: there is no interaction between observer and observed.

This passive observation of experience is a direct reflection of Hardy's view of the world, as a place in which there is much to be endured, and little that can be changed. The philosophical bases for this view Hardy spelled out in many places (most elaborately, of course, in *The Dynasts*); but in "Afterwards" he was content to leave the philosophy implicit in the imagery, and this indirectness is one of the excellences of the poem. It is an excellence, however, only because the imagery focuses precisely on the points of time and change which are the points of the poem (as of so many of Hardy's poems). A sense of time runs through the poem—the "when" of each stanza is set up in the first line, and the rest of the stanza develops an action appropriate to that moment. The actions are themselves momentary—new leaves move, a hawk glides down, a hedgehog scurries past. Nothing that the observer can do can fix these brief moments, or preserve the creatures that act in them; he can seem to fix them in his memory, but, since he shares their mortality, this fixity is only apparent. Because he alone of mortal creatures is conscious of his mortality, he cherishes his observations of the world he loves, but because he has no defense against change and death, his love is touched with melancholy. Only the stars remain after he has been stilled, and they remain as mysteries.

Some of Hardy's poems contain only a single image; others (like "Afterwards") are nearly all imagery. (I say *nearly* all, for there is no Hardy poem which is imagistic in the T. E. Hulme-Amy Lowell sense—there is always, on the surface or under it, the groping for the meaning of the experience which gives Hardy his depth.) In either case, the function of imagery is the same—the individual image takes its place in a pattern which is a microcosm of the universal conflict that Hardy saw as the nature of things. In "A Broken Appointment" the only images are in the line "And marching Time drew on, and wore me numb," and in the phrase "time-torn man"; the rest is a monologue of quiet regret which is essentially abstract. But these two images are crucial to the poem; they inject destructive actuality into an otherwise non-physical poem, and give tension and poignancy to the quiet endurance which the speaking voice manifests. They also modify each other, since Time in the first image is, at least superficially, the time spent waiting for the woman who doesn't come, while in the second it is Time in larger terms, Time-the-destroyer, Hardy's old enemy, with whom the woman is now in league. So love becomes time's accomplice in the long abrasion which was, for Hardy, life.

"A Merrymaking in Question" is a poem which is nearly all imagery, and which offers a simple example of the way in which Hardy sets one antinomial term against another in balanced stanzas:

> "I will get a new string for my fiddle,
>   And call to the neighbours to come,
> And partners shall dance down the middle
>   Until the old pewter-wares hum:
>   And we'll sip the mead, cyder, and rum!"
>
> From the night came the oddest of answers;
>   A hollow wind, like a bassoon,
> And headstones all ranged up as dancers,
>   And cypresses droning a croon,
>   And gurgoyles that mouthed to the tune.
>
>   (*Collected Poems*, pp. 436-37)

The pattern is very clear here. The first stanza is an arrangement of joyous images as uncomplicated as a C major chord. The second stanza makes that simplicity complex and dissonant by "mismarrying" the imagery of dancing and singing to images of death. It is the oddest of answers in that it is not an answer at all (Hardy's poems rarely are). It does not resolve anything—it simply juxtaposes the expectation of joy and the reality of death in images which force us to relate the two.

While the imagery of Hardy's novels is often similar in detail to that of the poems (the same images of darkness and death, of suffering creatures, of weather and seasons appear), it is generally weaker—more diffuse, decorative ("Queen of the Night," that great patch of purple in *The Return of the Native,* is a good example of bad practice), self-consciously literary and arty, and a little timid. Hardy conveniently left us a perfect opportunity for comparison—the same image in prose and in poetry. The prose is from the *Native*:

Before him stretched the long, laborious road, dry, empty, and white. It was quite open to the heath on each side, and bisected that vast dark surface like the parting-line on a head of black hair, diminishing and bending away on the furthest horizon (p. 8).

The poem is "The Roman Road":

>The Roman Road runs straight and bare
>As the pale parting-line in hair
>Across the heath. . . .   (*Collected Poems,* p. 248)

The prose image, you will notice, is preceded by a series of descriptive adjectives, like a photograph of a scene set beside a landscape painting of it, to explain what the whole thing is about. Hardy's prose imagery is often weakened in this way, as well as by the clutter of philosophizing remarks which he was prone to insert into his imaginative writing to drive home the point of it all. The poetic image, on the other hand, is direct and economical; it is less descriptive in that it restricts the comparison to straightness and bareness, but it is stronger for this characteristic, since it does not force upon us the grotesque proposition that a road really looks like a parting-line, as the prose image does.

This weakness of prose imagery (and I don't mean to suggest that it is all this weak) is probably partly the result of the form—a man engaged in filling three volumes a year is likely to be expansive and repetitious. It may also, perhaps, be explained as simply another manifestation of Hardy's willingness to write to the taste and expectations of his Victorian novel-reading public, and to explain the hard bits as he went.

But if the imagery of the novels reveals Hardy's weaknesses, the imagery of his poems reveals his strengths: his steady, uncomforted, ironic vision; his fidelity to that vision as the one legitimate motive force in his poetry; his sense of structure in the balancing of his two worlds; and his meticulous eye, not simply for detail (for he was not a word-painter), but for the significant, emotionally charged detail. There are weaknesses, too, for Hardy was as capable of vagueness and conventionality and circumlocution in his imagery as he was in his diction (the two are not, in fact, entirely separable—one sin generally produces the other). But the final, total impression which the imagery of the poems creates is of an extraordinary sensibility, confined by a relentless pessimism into a narrow channel, limited in range and yet, within that range, honest, perceptive, and sometimes magnificent.

8

The Question of Development

So FAR THESE remarks, like most criticisms of Hardy, have tacitly assumed that his poetry is all of a piece, one solid mass of verse expressing a sensibility at a single stage of development. For critics, Hardy has had no poetic periods—one does not speak of early Hardy or late Hardy, or of the London or Max Gate period, but simply of Hardy, as of a poetic monolith. This seems odd when one recalls that he wrote poetry longer than any other major English poet: "Domicilium" is dated "between 1857 and 1860"; "Seeing the Moon Rise" is dated August, 1927. One might expect that in a poetic career of seventy-odd years, some changes in style and method would have occurred, some development taken place.

This is not, however, the case, and development is a term which we can apply to Hardy only in a very limited sense. In a time when poetic style, and poetic belief as well, seem in a state of continual flux, Hardy stands out as a poet of almost perverse consistency. Though he struggled with philosophy all his life, he never got much beyond the pessimism of his twenties; the "sober opinion" of his letter to Noyes, written when Hardy was eighty years old, is essentially that of his first "philosophical" notebook entry, made when he was twenty-five: "The world does not despise us: it only neglects us" (*Early Life,* p. 63). And though in his later years he revised his poems many times, the revisions did not alter the essential nature of the style which he had established before he was thirty; so that, while it usually is easy to recognize a poem by Hardy, it is difficult to date one.

There is only one sense in which it is valid to talk about Hardy's development: he did develop toward a more consistent and more effective control of that tone which we recognize as uniquely his. There is only one Hardy style, but in the earlier poems that style is only intermittently evident, and when it is not, the style is the style of another poet, or of the fashion of the time. In the later poems, however, the personal tone predominates. The bad early poems are bad Shakespeare or bad Swinburne; the bad late poems are bad Hardy.

There are two ways of getting at a poet's development: through his dated poems, and through the revisions which he made in later editions of his work. About a quarter of Hardy's poems carry an appended date line, usually the year of completion, but sometimes inclusive years ("1908-1910") or two separate dates when Hardy worked on the poem ("1905 and 1926") or an approximate date ("During the War"). These dates are virtually the only clues we have to the chronology of the poems, since the separate volumes are neither chronological within themselves nor in relation to each other. With the exception of *Satires of Circumstance,* each volume contains dated poems ranging over several decades (*Winter Words* spans sixty-one years); the internal organization rarely has any chronological order, except in obvious groups like the "Poems of Pilgrimage," the "Poems of 1912-13," and the war poems.

From the dated poems we can venture certain conclusions about Hardy's career in poetry, always remembering that conclusions based on a fraction of the whole must remain tentative. The dated poems suggest that while Hardy's concern with poetry may have been constant, his production was not. He had two productive periods, one in the late 1860's, the other in the decade from 1910 to 1920 (half of the dated poems are from the latter period, and these alone total about one-tenth of all Hardy's poems). There was one sterile period: only one poem is dated between 1872 and 1882 and, except for the poems written on the trip to Italy in 1887, very few from 1882 to 1890.

The dated poems also give us an idea of the degree to which Hardy drew upon past productions for his various volumes, and therefore probably are an indication of the amount of poetry he was writing at the time. *Poems of the Past and the Present* and *Time's Laughingstocks,* both published while Hardy was at work on *The Dynasts,* draw heavily on poems written before 1900. *Satires of Circumstance* and *Moments of Vision,* coming during his most productive decade, are relatively self-contained; the former contains no poem dated before 1909-10—that is, no poem from a period covered by a previous volume—and the latter has only a few such. The last three volumes are again more dependent on the past, as Hardy's creative powers declined in his old age.

These observations about Hardy's productivity tally with the details of his life as we know them. The first productive period came when he was considering poetry as a vocation, before he had decided to write fiction for a living (in his note for *Who's Who* he wrote that he "wrote verses 1865-1868; gave up verse for prose, 1868-70; but resumed it later"). During the poetically sterile years he was writing novels at the rate of almost one a year and was, in addition, burdened with bad health (he spent six months in bed in 1881, too ill to do more than work slowly and painfully at *A Laodicean*). Two entries in the *Early Life* support the assumption that during this period Hardy had virtually suspended the writing of poetry. Mrs. Hardy records that "... at the end of November [1881] he makes a note of an intention to resume poetry as soon as possible" (*Early Life,* p. 188); and on Christmas Day, 1890, Hardy wrote: "While thinking of resuming 'the viewless wings of poesy' before dawn this morning, new horizons seemed to open, and worrying pettinesses to disappear" (*Early Life,* p. 302). There are more poems dated in the 1890's than in the '80's— Hardy had apparently resumed the viewless wings as he decreased the volume of his fiction—but none in 1891, the year of *Tess*, and only one in 1895, the year of *Jude*. After 1895 the number increases, and in the next thirty years there is only one year for which there is no dated poem—1903, when Hardy was at work on *The Dynasts*.

The second productive period, the decade from 1910 to 1920, can be related to three events: the completion of *The Dynasts* in 1909, which left Hardy free of pressure for the first time in forty years; the death of Emma Hardy in 1912, which had a profound emotional effect on Hardy for which he found release in poetry; and the First World War. It may seem strange that a poet should come to full fruition in his seventies, but we have it on Hardy's own authority that "... he was a child till he was sixteen, a youth till he was five-and-twenty, and a young man till he was nearly fifty" (*Early Life*, p. 42). We may carry this sequence one step further and say that at seventy he was a poet at the height of his powers, wanting only the impetus of two tragedies, one personal, the other national, to loose those powers in poetry.

Hardy's two productive decades were separated by forty years, yet between them he developed only in that he became more steadily himself—it was a narrowing, not an expanding process. Like a wise gardener, Hardy pruned away the Shakespearian sonnets and songs, and the elements of meter and poetic diction to which his personal style was not suited, and let the main stock of his talent flourish. The range of the later poetry is considerably narrower, but the number of successful poems is far greater.

We can see the general characteristics of the earlier decade if we look at two poems of very different qualities: "Revulsion" (1866) and "Neutral Tones" (1867).

REVULSION

Though I waste watches framing words to fetter
Some unknown spirit to mine in clasp and kiss,
Out of the night there looms a sense 'twere better
To fail obtaining whom one fails to miss.

For winning love we win the risk of losing,
And losing love is as one's life were riven;
It cuts like contumely and keen ill-using
To cede what was superfluously given.

Let me then never feel the fateful thrilling
That devastates the love-worn wooer's frame,
The hot ado of fevered hopes, the chilling
That agonizes disappointed aim!
So may I live no junctive law fulfilling,
And my heart's table bear no woman's name.

(*Collected Poems*, p. 11)

NEUTRAL TONES

We stood by a pond that winter day,
And the sun was white, as though chidden of God,
And a few leaves lay on the starving sod;
    —They had fallen from an ash, and were gray.

Your eyes on me were as eyes that rove
Over tedious riddles of years ago;
And some words played between us to and fro
    On which lost the more by our love.
The smile on your mouth was the deadest thing
Alive enough to have strength to die;
And a grin of bitterness swept thereby
    Like an ominous bird a-wing. . . .

Since then, keen lessons that love deceives,
And wrings with wrong, have shaped to me
Your face, and the God-curst sun, and a tree,
    And a pond edged with grayish leaves.

(*Collected Poems*, p. 9)

There is not much to be said for "Revulsion." Like about half of the 1860-70 poems, it is a sonnet on a conventional theme—the unhappiness of love. Almost anyone could have written it; it is competent in the sense that it makes a coherent statement without violating the rules of the sonnet form, but it is entirely undistinguished and entirely unlike Hardy. The language is the conventional language of the form; there is no phrase or image that sounds like Hardy or that is striking enough to give individuality to the poem. It is smoother than Hardy usually is, but with the smoothness of anonymity. It is obviously a young man's poem, written out of books and not out of experience; it asserts emotion without evoking it—that is to say, it is sentimental. There are many such competently anonymous performances among the earlier poems.

"Neutral Tones" we immediately recognize as a fine poem in Hardy's most characteristic style: the plain but not quite colloquial language, the hard, particular, colorless images, the slightly odd stanza-form, the dramatic handling of the occasion, the refusal to resolve the issue—all these we have seen in Hardy's best poems. The poem does not distort the syntax of ordinary speech nor draw on exotic sources of diction, yet it is obviously *not* ordinary speech—only Hardy would say "a grin of bitterness swept thereby/Like an ominous bird a-wing," or "wrings with wrong," or would describe a winter sun as "God-curst."

The details of the setting of "Neutral Tones" are not, strictly speaking, metaphorical, but they combine to create a mood which is appropriate both to a dismal winter day and to the end of love, and in this way love and weather, the emotions and the elements, symbolize each other in a way that is common to many of Hardy's best poems ("Weathers," "The Darkling Thrush," and "During Wind and Rain," for example) and to some moving passages in the novels as well (*Far From the Madding Crowd* is full of scenes constructed in this way).

"Neutral Tones" is an excellent example of Hardy's mature style, drawn from his earliest productive period; I cite it as evidence that he did not develop through new styles as he grew older (as Yeats did), but that he simply learned to use better what he already had. In the poem we recognize and acknowledge one man's sense of the world; if it is somber, it is also precise, and the precision lends authority to the vision. In "Revulsion," on the other hand, the pessimism is a case not proven; the poem offers nothing to persuade us of the speaker's right to speak as he does. In the 1860-70 decade there are many poems like "Revulsion," but there is only one "Neutral Tones." Hardy was not Hardy very often.

The "Poems of 1912-13" offer a good example of Hardy's style as it was manifested in the later productive decade. These are the poems Hardy wrote after the death of his first wife; they compose a painful elegy to what might have been, to a marriage that began with a promise of happiness, and ended in long years of suffering and hatred. Hardy obviously felt that these poems were peculiarly personal and private; he sometimes called them "an expiation," and he would not allow them to be published in periodicals. They are the only poems that he rearranged as a group between their first appearance (in *Satires of Circumstance*) and the publication of the *Collected Poems*.

The elegiac tone is Hardy's natural tone of voice, and it is not surprising that the 1912-13 poems are consistently and unmistakably his. The view is always toward the past, but the mood is not quite nostalgic—Hardy would not allow sentiment to soften his sense of the irredeemable pastness of the past, and the eternal deadness of the dead. The poems are, the epigraph tells us, the "traces of an ancient flame"; the fire of love is dead, and Hardy stands, as the speaker does in the last poem of the sequence, over the burnt circle of charred sticks, and thinks of past happiness and present grief, honest and uncomforted. This absolute honesty is in part a function of the style, which by its harshness, awkwardness, and eccentricity—all the traits we usually find in Hardy's style—gives the impression of being absolutely determined by an undeviating fidelity to the event as it was.

We have already examined one of the best poems in the sequence, "The Voice": the "undeviating fidelity" is manifested here both in the content of the poem and in its form. In the first stanza Hardy carefully explains that the woman had changed during their relationship, and for the worse, but also that at the beginning their "day was fair"—neither sentimental nostalgia nor bitterness is allowed to distort the truth. In the third stanza he admits that the woman is gone forever and that the voice he hears cannot be hers; he declines, as he does in all the elegies, the comforts of a belief in immortality. Formally, the most striking thing about the poem, as I remarked before, is the way in which the stanza form changes at the end, as the poem shifts from memory and imagination to present reality; here the meter becomes in a sense metaphorical, changing as the mood of the poem changes.

In "The Voice" the style is both characteristically Hardy's and entirely at the service of an honest statement of the truth of the occasion, the total grief that comes with total, uncomforted loss. Style and occasion strengthen each other. It is obviously putting it too crudely to say that Hardy needed a death in the family for poetic reasons, but there is some truth in the suggestion. As experience deepened his sense of the radical disparities of existence, of the inexorability of time, and of the meaninglessness and inevitability of suffering, he came more and more to write in one mood. The death of his wife provided him with materials of the deepest personal significance and immediacy which were dramatically appropriate to that mood, and which could be powerfully expressed within the limitations of the Hardy style. Hence the odd fact that the "Poems of 1912-13" seem at once Hardy's most personal utterances and his most typical poems; in them, the style and the moment meet.

Nevertheless, we must recognize that the style of the later

period differs from that of the earlier period only in that it is more constant and more sure. Insofar as "Revulsion" represents a style, that style fades out, but the style of "Neutral Tones" is essentially that of "The Voice," and continues to be Hardy's primary style to the end of his life. I have for convenience taken two decades from Hardy's poetic career and called them "early" and "late," but the difference between them is only relative, and the change from one to the other (principally a matter of abandoning alien styles) came about slowly. It was pretty well completed by 1910, however, and, as I shall argue in the next chapter, *The Dynasts* was probably the stabilizing factor.

Once Hardy's style became fixed, changes in his verse became retrospective—revisions of earlier poems to bring them up to the level of the later ones. The nature of the standards involved, the principles of Hardy's style, can be inferred from the directions that these revisions took.

We may assume that Hardy made his first revisions soon after the completion of *The Dynasts,* probably in 1911 or 1912. The occasion was the preparation of the Wessex Edition of his works; since we know that he was correcting proofs of the novels in April, 1912 (*Later Years,* p. 151), we may reasonably place the revisions of the poems at about the same time. Only *Wessex Poems* and *Poems of the Past and the Present* are included in this edition, but for these two collections the job of revision was a thorough one, so thorough that two-thirds of the revised poems were not altered again.

The poems were reworked for a second time for the *Selected Poems* of 1916. Selections from both the volumes included in the Wessex Edition were used, plus poems from *Time's Laughingstocks* and *Satires of Circumstance,* and a few later included in *Moments of Vision*. A number of the poems were extensively revised for the first time for this volume; other revisions were slight (particularly of poems previously revised for the Wessex Edition). Many of the poems were only half-revised, that is they contain some, but not all of the revisions which appear in the final versions in *Collected Poems*. A few contain revisions which do not appear elsewhere; a number of titles, for example, were simplified for this edition and later restored to their original form, and a stanza was omitted from one poem of the Boer War to make the poem applicable to the First World War.

A third, and most important revision was made between 1916 and the publication of the English edition of the *Collected Poems* in 1919. This revision is most thorough, and may have occupied Hardy over much of the intervening three years. He also considerably reworked *Late Lyrics and Earlier* between 1922, when it appeared, and 1925, when it was included in the *Collected Poems,* and he even made slight revisions in some poems in *Human Shows* (1925), the last volume to appear during his lifetime.

The number of poems revised varies as one might expect, from volume to volume, being greatest in the earliest volume and least in the last one. Two-thirds of the *Wessex Poems* were revised at one time or another; in the later volumes the percentage of poems altered decreases fairly steadily: *Poems of the Past and the Present,* 50 per cent; *Time's Laughingstocks,* 22 per cent; *Satires of Circumstance,* 40 per cent; *Moments of Vision,* 40 per cent; *Late Lyrics and Earlier,* 7 per cent; *Human Shows,* 3 per cent. The amount of revision in individual poems varies in roughly the same way: that is, it is greatest in *Wessex Poems* and least in *Human Shows*.

But even the most extensive changes involve only portions of poems; Hardy revised, but he did not rewrite, in the way that Yeats, for example, did. In only a few instances is the sense of the poem changed, and where this does occur, it does so only because the tone is obviously the important element in the poem and is not affected by the sense change, as in the following example from *Late Lyrics*:

> HER APOTHEOSIS
> "Secretum meum mihi"
> (FADED WOMAN'S SONG)
>
> There was a spell of leisure
> No record vouches when;
> With honours, praises, pleasure
> To womankind from men.
>
> But no such lures bewitched me,
> No hand was stretched to raise,
> No gracious gifts enriched me,
> No voices sang my praise.
>
> Yet an iris at that season
> Amid the accustomed slight
> From denseness, dull unreason,
> Ringed me with living light.
>
> (*Late Lyrics*, p. 229)

The *Collected Poems* version reads:

> There were years vague of measure
> Needless the asking when;
> No honours, praises, pleasure
> Reached common maids from men.
>
> And hence no lures bewitched them,
> No hand was stretched to raise,
> No gracious gifts enriched them,
> No voices sang their praise.

> Yet an iris at that season
> Amid the accustomed slight
> From denseness, dull unreason,
> Ringed me with living light.
>
> (*Collected Poems*, p. 634)

The sense of the first two stanzas is entirely changed in the revision—the relation of "common maids" to "honours, praises, pleasure" is reversed. But the central emotional fact remains the same: the faded woman was once transformed, presumably by love. The poem exists for the image of the third stanza, for which the two preceding stanzas provide an introduction. The introduction is altered, the way into the poem is changed, but the core is constant, and any introduction will do which brings us to that core.

Even in a revision as extensive as "Her Apotheosis" the form of the poem is not changed. Form is rarely an affective element of supreme importance in Hardy's poems; more often it seems accidental, a framework chosen at random, with no particular adjustment made to the demands of the poem. As a consequence, there are many weak poems padded or cramped to fit an inadequate form, and some of the revisions are obvious attempts to cope with the inadequacies. Here are a few lines, typical in stanzaic form, from the *Wessex Poems* version of "Her Death and After":

> ... and to shun his nod
> By her hallowed sod
> I went from the tombs among
>
> To the Cirque of the Gladiators which faced—
> That haggard mark of Imperial Rome,
> Whose Pagan echoes mock the chime
> Of our Christian Time—
> It was void, and I inward clomb.
>
> (*Wessex Poems*, p. 103)

Hardy apparently felt the last line to be superfluous to the sense of the stanza; he altered it three times in an effort to draw it back into the stanza, and to give the stanza unity in itself and in relation to the poem as a whole. In the Wessex Edition (vol. 19, p. 50) the line reads:

> And I drew to its bank and clomb.

For the *Selected Poems* (p. 175) Hardy changed it to

> From its hollows of turf and loam

and in the *Collected Poems* (p. 36) to

> From its hollows of chalk and loam.

In the last two revisions the dash at the end of the fourth line is deleted, so that the last line is included in the parenthesis beginning "that haggard mark." The final version is a slight improvement; it fits the rhyme scheme, it avoids the archaic *clomb,* and it completes the stanza with a finality that the first version did not have. But it is still close to doggerel, because there is nothing left to say— the stanza is too big for the content, and the last line remains a superfluous appendage.

Hardy apparently could not alter the form of a poem, once he was committed to it. If it seemed inadequate to the occasion, the most he seemed capable of was adding or deleting a stanza. These revisions are not frequent, but they have a certain importance in that they indicate two of Hardy's major aims in revising. All the added stanzas occur in narrative poems and have a single, simple function—increased clarity of narration. Of the deletions, a few were determined by topical considerations—the necessity, for example, of making Boer War poems do for World War I, or reducing the pacifist internationalism of a pre-war poem for wartime publication. Others are more significant, for the deletions eliminate specific, explanatory material, and shift the poem toward the mood of vague, unspecified disaster which informs so much of Hardy's lyric verse. "The Caged Goldfinch" appeared in *Moments of Vision* in three stanzas:

> Within a churchyard, on a recent grave,
>   I saw a little cage
> That jailed a goldfinch. All was silence save
>   Its hops from stage to stage.
>
> There was inquiry in its wistful eye,
>   And once it tried to sing;
> Of him or her who placed it there, and why,
>   No one knew anything.
>
> True, a woman was found drowned the day ensuing,
>   And some at times averred
> The grave to be her false one's, who when wooing
>   Gave her the bird.
>
>   (*Moments of Vision*, p. 129)

For the *Collected Poems* Hardy dropped the third stanza (apparently someone had explicated the last line for him) and strengthened the poem. In the first version it is simply another of Hardy's dreary little tragedies of false lovers; in the second it is essentially a juxtaposition of disparate images—bird and grave—to produce a kind of minor chord of emotions. To specify details is to destroy this chord; the second version says all that can be said.

In these revisions Hardy seems to have had two general aims: he added to the narrative poems for the sake of clarity —elaboration where it was necessary, in an added stanza or an added line, simplification of statement elsewhere; he deleted passages from the lyrics because his aim there was maximum emotional effect—he revised away from the obvious limitations of the specific, toward the characteristic individual tone, and the implied situation.

Formal revisions are not, however, the most frequent expressions of these aims. Hardy's major technical interest was verbal—texture, not form—and changes in language and syntax account for the majority of his revisions. One cannot formulate any simple rule to explain these revisions, for Hardy was revising by ear, not by theory; the revisions are usually felt as improvements, but they are improvements in several directions.

One can, however, make certain broad generalizations. In his revisions of the early volumes, particularly in the narrative poems, Hardy tended to eliminate oddness in favor of colloquial speech. Archaisms and dialect words are translated into standard English—*peäir* to *pair, en* to *him, vlanker* to *flapping, glode* to *slid;* poetic diction is eliminated —*wight* becomes *wooer, for aye* becomes *for good;* grave accents and poetic contractions disappear; and certain coinages are changed—*have unbe* to *not have be, crescive* to *crescent, outgave* to *pronounced*. Here, as an example of how these changes look in context, are two stanzas from Hardy's early, bad poem, "My Cicely." In the *Wessex Poems* version (pp. 126-28):

> And by Weatherbury Castle, and therence
> > Through Casterbridge bore I
> To tomb her whose light, in my deeming
> > Extinguished had He.
> . . . .
> I shuddered, said nothing, and wandered
> > To shades of green laurel:
> Too ghastly had grown those first tidings
> > So brightsome of blee.

And in the *Collected Poems* version (pp. 46-43):

> And by Weatherbury Castle, and thencefrom
> > Through Casterbridge held I
> Still on, to entomb her my mindsight
> > Saw stretched pallidly.
>
> . . . .
>
> I shuddered, said nothing, and wandered
> > To shades of green laurel:
> More ghastly than death were these tidings
> > Of life's irony.

The revised stanzas are not poetry of a very high quality, but they are improvements over the earlier version, and the direction of the improvements is clear enough.

In the later volumes, roughly from *Time's Laughingstocks* (1909), the revisions take a somewhat different form. Here one finds Hardy reinserting his characteristic oddnesses, though avoiding the "gauche unshrinking mismarriages" of early poems like "My Cicely." Apparently he had learned the limits of his eccentricity (it is worth noting that *Time's Laughingstocks* is the first volume to follow the completion of *The Dynasts*, where Hardy's experiments in eccentricity are most evident). Here are a few changes characteristic of the later revisions: *husband* to *life-mate*, *attentive* to *mute and museful*, *possessor* to *bed-winner*, *tortured* to *rafted*, *family feature* to *years-heired feature*, and *surpassed* to *outpriced*. There are many more revisions of the same order. These changes sharpen one's sense of the situation and heighten one's awareness of the transmuting personality of the poet, but they do so without recourse to archaism or extreme neologism.

The point can only be argued when individual words are seen in context; but perhaps one example will give some indication of how they work. The stanza is from "The Moth-Signal"; it reads like this in *Satires of Circumstance* (p. 192):

> She rose, and, little heeding,
>   Her husband then went on
> With his attentive reading
>   In the annals of ages gone.

and like this in the *Collected Poems* (p. 369):

> She rose, and little heeding,
>   Her lifemate then went on
> With his mute and museful reading
>   In the annals of ages gone.

Husband merely indicates a legal relationship, but *life-mate* points to the terms of the relationship and underscores the ironic situation of "one whose marriage troth is/Shattered as potsherds are." *Mute and museful* adds qualities of character to the fact that the husband is attending to his reading rather than to his wife, and suggests something about the marriage. The whole stanza, in revision, has the tone of Hardy's voice, as it does not in the first version.

In the later volumes a consistent sharpening of verbs and verbal elements is also apparent—Hardy changed *bird flies* to *bird wings*, *year was out* to *year ebbed out*, *reflecting* to *glassing*, *passed* to *pilgrimed*. These small changes are all in the direction of greater exactness, but not at the expense of the personal speaking voice—most of them one would recognize as typical Hardyisms. Because sharp verbal action is a dominant element in Hardy's style, these revisions are important as indications that Hardy was aware of his own strengths and was revising toward them.

The changes which Hardy made in syntax are generally in the same direction as the verbal changes—away from the "poetic" and the grotesque, but not entirely away from the idiosyncratic. Most of the revisions in syntax simply eliminate noun-adjective inversions, and most occur in the early poems, where such inversions are frequent. I will set a few examples in order, the first in each case being the original version, the second the revised version from the *Collected Poems*:

> At Casterbridge experience keen
> Of many loves had she
> > (*Wessex Poems*, p. 108)
>
> And few in Casterbridge had seen
> More loves of sorts than she
> > (*Collected Poems*, p. 38)

> Moments the mightiest pass uncalendared
> > (*Poems of the Past and the Present*, p. 1)
>
> The mightiest moments pass uncalendared
> > (*Collected Poems*, p. 77)

> To work where they were placed rude men were meant
> > (*Poems of the Past and the Present*, p. 180)
>
> Rude men should work where placed, and be content
> > (*Collected Poems*, p. 140)

> Be candid would I willingly
> > (*Time's Laughingstocks*, p. 74)
>
> I would be candid willingly.
> > (*Collected Poems*, p. 214)

All of these syntactical revisions smooth out roughnesses which had no clear poetic function; none eliminates anything that could be regarded as characteristic of Hardy's style. Such inversions are a stock part of a "poetic" style, and Hardy's style without them is more plainly his own.

Certain revisions cannot be classified as changes in variety of diction or in syntax, but are simply verbal improvements within the limits of standard English; some of the most successful revisions are of this sort. Sometimes only one word is changed, as in the last stanza of "In Time of 'The Breaking of Nations,'" which first read like this:

> Yonder a maid and her wight
>   Come whispering by:
> War's annals will cloud into night
>   Ere their story die.
>
> <div align="right">(<i>Moments of Vision</i>, p. 232)</div>

In the *Collected Poems* Hardy changed *cloud* to *fade*. *Cloud* creates an inexact image in context—the relation of cloud to night, for example, is arbitrary, and the significance of "war's annals" is not clear. *Fade,* on the other hand, carries the image of slow dissolution which is relevant to the context; war can be imaged, without straining, as the blood-red sunset which will fade into time's darkness. *Fade,* occurring here in terms of sunset, brings the weight of cyclic pattern to the stanza, and strengthens the theme of permanence and change which is the point of the poem.

Hardy's eye was primarily on the language, but here and there lines which originally were flat and prosy, or metronomically regular, were strengthened by the changes in meter which verbal changes necessitated. The last line of "During Wind and Rain" shows such an improvement:

> Down their chiselled names the rain-drop ploughs
> <div align="right">(<i>Moments of Vision</i>, p. 138)</div>
> Down their carved names the rain-drop ploughs
> <div align="right">(<i>Collected Poems</i>, p. 465)</div>

Chiselled forces the line into a sing-song alternation of stressed and unstressed syllables; *carved* throws two stresses together, and prepares the ear to hear the last three syllables of the line as equally stressed. Consequently the line is slower, the image lingered over in a way which is right for the termination of a meditative poem.

One might add, for the sake of completeness, a few other minor kinds of revision which Hardy made. He corrected grammar and punctuation—changed *like* to *as* and *which* to *that,* changed semicolons to colons, and inserted and removed dashes. None of these revisions changes the sense of the poems at all, but they do show the meticulousness with which Hardy went about improving his work, and setting it in the final order in which it reaches us.

Hardy's later poems are closer to standard, conversational English than are the early ones—less dependent on inherited poetic diction, archaisms and dialect, less tortured in syntax—but they are not in the language of common speech. Nobody talks quite like a Hardy poem; but then, nobody talks poetry. The problem of style which Hardy faced must confront anyone who endeavors to break away from conventional poetic statement in the direction of more personal, more direct expression. Wordsworth faced it in his "Preface," and resolved it with a qualifying clause:

> The principal object, then, proposed in these poems was to choose incidents and situations from common life, and to relate or describe them, throughout, as far as was possible in a selection of language really used by men, and, at the same time, to throw over them a certain colouring of imagination, whereby ordinary things should be presented to the mind in an unusual aspect.[52]

The last clause sounds rather like Hardy's goal, "the other side of common emotions"; it is this element of difference, the "unusual aspect," that is likely to make a poem, in Hardy as in Wordsworth.

That unusual aspect appeared in Hardy's poems from the beginning, but it took him some forty years to learn to control it, or even, perhaps, to know when he had it and when he didn't. For though Hardy was as self-conscious as a poet could be, he was not self-critical. We never find in his notes on his craft a sense of personal failure—he speaks occasionally of his best poems, but never of his worst. He does not speak of his own works, as Auden does of *The Orators,* as "a case of the fair notion fatally injured," nor does he, as Eliot does in *Poetry and Drama,* describe what he has learned from his own mistakes. Self-criticism was not a part of Hardy's nature, and without self-criticism a poet is not likely to develop beyond his natural gifts.

Hardy refined his natural gifts and learned to play more skillful variations on his themes, but he did not expand his vision or his method. The reason for this radical limitation is to be found, I think, in Hardy's philosophical problems. He could not find it in himself to hold man responsible for his actions or his fate; Crass Casualty, Chance, some Vast Imbecility were to blame. Philosophically, this view may be tenable, but poetically it is almost fatal; Chance and Fate make poor Muses, and automatons, one would expect, make poor poets. Hardy was sometimes a good poet because he was an inconsistent one, but his philosophy did not allow him to develop as another, less intransigently honest philosophy might have. He could not remake himself (as Yeats did); he had to be content with himself as he was.

9

The Dynasts *as an Example*

SOONER OR LATER the artist involved with questions of meaning and belief (and this probably means every major artist) must feel the need to impose upon his ideas the complex organization which a long work requires. At the same time the conditions of belief in our time raise special problems for the artist with such intentions; he can neither assume a core of beliefs common to himself and his audience nor adopt the long forms which artists have traditionally used for such statements. Consequently, the long works which modern writers have produced have tended to be private, difficult, and eccentric—*Ulysses, The Cantos, The Waste Land,* and "The Comedian as the Letter C" have these qualities in common, if they have nothing else. None is epic in a traditional sense, though all have epic elements; none has a traditional hero; none depends on or asserts traditional values. They are epics for an age in which epic action is impossible.

The Dynasts is Hardy's venture into this realm of the modern epic. But for our purposes it is something more than that; it is Hardy's great effort to put his philosophical and poetic principles into practice on the largest possible scale. That tremendous scale makes *The Dynasts* useful as a test both of his principles and of the judgments we have thus far made of them.

Hardy must have sensed early in his career that lyric and anecdotal poetry could not give full and satisfactory expression to his thought—that he required a massive structure to support a modern epic. For over twenty years he pondered the shape that it should take, and made tentative, speculative entries in his notebooks. It appeared at last as *The Dynasts,* his most ambitious philosophical statement, in his most original form—the "epic-drama."

Some version of epic was, as Hardy saw from the first, the only possible vehicle for the philosophical statement that he intended. Traditionally, the epic has served didactic, philosophical, or religious purposes, embodying in a mythical history the values of the culture which produced it. In the epic hero it offers an image of the human potentialities implicit in those values. And it freely employs supernatural actors to dramatize the relation of man (in the person of the epic hero) to the controlling forces of the universe. It offers a canvas vast enough for a comprehensive statement within a single form, and it is unhampered by the restrictions of realism or probability.

In all these characteristics, the epic suited Hardy's aims, as the forms he had previously tried did not. The "philosophical" lyrics, as we have seen, could rarely support the weight of didacticism imposed upon them—the human figures, even those in the dramatic ballads, are too pallid to have much symbolic force, and the supernatural actors, when they appear, are generally felt to be extraneous. Even the great novels show in their defects the restrictions of a limited range, and of the demand for probability and realism implicit in the form as Hardy used it (most adverse criticisms of the novels are in these terms).

From the first, Hardy thought of his long poem as epic in scope, though not in form. The first entry[53] in the notebooks relative to *The Dynasts,* dated May, 1875, reads: "Mem: A Ballad of the Hundred Days. Then another of Moscow. Others of earlier campaigns—forming altogether an Iliad of Europe from 1789 to 1815" (*Early Life,* p. 140). Six years later he entered this note: "A Homeric Ballad, in which Napoleon is a sort of Achilles, to be written" (*Early Life,* p. 191). The idea of the ballad-form did not survive—Hardy required, as he came to realize, "a larger canvas"—but the concept of an "Iliad of Europe" with Napoleon as the epic hero did.

The choice of subject matter was, given Hardy's habits of mind, almost inevitable. Hardy explains in the Preface to *The Dynasts* that

The choice of such a subject was mainly due to three accidents of locality. It chanced that the writer was familiar with a part of England that lay within hail of the watering-place in which King George the Third had his favourite summer residence during the war with the first Napoleon, and where he was visited by ministers and others who bore the weight of English affairs on their more or less competent shoulders at that stressful time. Secondly, this district, being also near the coast which had echoed with rumours of invasion in their intensest form while the descent threatened, was formerly animated by memories and traditions of the desperate military preparations for that contingency. Thirdly, the same countryside happened to include the village which was the birthplace of Nelson's flag-captain at Trafalgar (p. vii).

It is true that, without these local materials, Hardy's epic would have been different in many particulars; but it would still, I think, have been an Iliad of Europe, and Napoleon would still have played his role as "a sort of Achilles." The notebook entries regarding *The Dynasts* range over some thirty years, but they make no mention of Dorset or of Captain Hardy; they deal primarily with two concerns: the form which the history of Napoleon and the Hundred Days should take, and the philosophical content which that history could be made to bear. It is oversimplifying to explain the attraction which Napoleon and the French Revolution had for Hardy as merely the result of "accidents of locality"; clearly the character and the events seemed to him to have a meaning which was relevant to his philosophic intentions.

Napoleon must have seemed to Hardy, and no doubt most modern readers would agree, the last figure in Western European history to whom epic stature could be ascribed. This point is important if we recall Hardy's view of the evolution of the "modern" personality (as set out in the first chapter of *The Return of the Native,* in the character of "Father Time" in *Jude,* and in various poems). If one accepts this notion of the *difference* of modern man, then one must find a modern hero, a modern epic story—classical themes will not do, because they represent man at a different stage of his evolution, less burdened by his own consciousness. (It is perhaps significant that Hardy rarely went outside his own century for material, and never successfully in a major work; *The Famous Tragedy of the Queen of Cornwall* is his most complete failure, partly because its traditional theme was not adaptable to Hardy's "modern" intentions.)

Furthermore, Hardy's Napoleon is, like other Hardy heroes, a man against the world—lonely and isolated even at the moment of his greatness. Hardy does not sentimentalize this isolation—Napoleon is not Childe Harold—but he does emphasize it, as he emphasized the isolation of Michael Henchard and Clym Yeobright and Jude Fawley. Man's alienation from men is an important aspect of Hardy's view of existence; it appears in the most characteristic situation of the lyric poems—the speaker alone, apart, out of place, "born out of due time"—as well as in the novels. Napoleon provided a dramatic example of the theme, a man lonely among multitudes.

Finally, Napoleon appears of all men the most self-determined, the absolute master of his fate, and this gives weight to the irony of a poem which was conceived in terms of "A spectral force seen acting in a man (e.g., Napoleon) and he acting under it—a pathetic sight—this compulsion" (*Later Years*, p. 227). An epic hero symbolizes the human condition as determined by the epic values. Napoleon stood, in Hardy's mind, as a dramatic symbol of man as Hardy saw him—struggling alone toward his own conception of his destiny—but helpless to alter his predetermined end. As darkness blots out Napoleon and the human scene for the last time in *The Dynasts*, the Spirit of the Years points the moral:

> Worthless these kneadings of thy narrow thought,
> Napoleon; gone thy opportunity!
> Such men as thou, who wade across the world
> To make an epoch, bless, confuse, appal,
> Are in the elemental ages' chart
> Like meanest insects on obscurest leaves
> But incidents and grooves of Earth's unfolding;
> Or as the brazen rod that stirs the fire
> Because it must.
>
> (*Dynasts*, III, VII, 9)

In Napoleon the paradox of human power and human helplessness, of will and necessity, emerges as a vast, cosmic irony.

Hardy's notes on *The Dynasts* follow, as I have said, two lines: the question of form and the question of philosophical content. Although Hardy saw the poem[54] from the first as epic in scope, he apparently never thought of employing the traditional epic form; the forms he considered were those most natural to his talent and to his vision—the ballad and the drama. At first he seemed uncertain as to which was preferable; in 1889 he recorded his decision:

For carrying out that idea of Napoleon, the Empress, Pitt, Fox, etc., I feel continually that I require a larger canvas ... A spectral tone must be adopted ... Royal ghosts ... Title: "A Drama of Kings" (*Early Life,* p. 290).

From this date on the form was determined; in 1891 he changed the title to "A Drama of the Times of the First Napoleon," and he later refers to the work as "the Napoleon drama"—there is no further reference to ballads. The term *epic* is curiously absent from the notes, and indeed Hardy did not come to call *The Dynasts* an "Epic-drama" until after it had been published.

On the question of philosophic content, however, Hardy's mind was clear from the beginning. The first notebook entry on the subject, dated 1881, outlines the philosophic scheme in substantially the form which it was to take twenty years later:

Mode for a historical Drama. Action mostly automatic; reflex movement, etc. Not the result of what is called *motive,* though always ostensibly so, even to the actors' own consciousness. Apply an enlargement of these theories to, say, "The Hundred Days"! (*Early Life,* p. 191).

The method by which this scheme could be made dramatic, however, was slower in evolving, and must have constituted the major problem of structure. Hardy began with a conviction that existing systems of belief were exhausted—not only as beliefs, but as materials for poetry:

> The old theologies [he wrote in an undated note] may or may not have worked for good in their time. But they will not bear stretching further in epic or dramatic art. The Greeks used up theirs: the Jews used up theirs: the Christians have used up theirs. So that one must make an independent plunge, embodying the real, if only temporary, thought of the age (*Later Years*, p. 104).[55]

Circumstances seemed to him to force upon him an act of creation not required of earlier epic poets—he had first to create his own theology.

His "independent plunge" was not, however, as sudden as the remark above suggests. Hardy was personifying the forces which controlled his private world as early as 1866, when he wrote in "Hap":

> Crass Casualty obstructs the sun and rain,
> And dicing Time for gladness casts a moan.
> These purblind Doomsters had as readily strown
> Blisses about my pilgrimage as pain.
>
> (*Collected Poems*, p. 7)

Casualty and Time remain essentially the "Doomsters" of all his work, both poems and novels, though their names change, until they emerge in *The Dynasts* as The Immanent Will and The Spirit of the Years. In between, the motive force is called a Vast Imbecility, an Automaton, The President of the Immortals, and of course God (a term which is, for Hardy, a private personification of the mindless, indifferent force which propels the universe). Time is intermediately the Spinner of Years and the Time-Wraiths. A third term, Nature or "The Mother," is also present from the beginning; she seems to represent a pre-conscious evolutionary system, the physical world as it would work if man had not developed beyond expectations. Like the other spirits in Hardy's Olympus, she is powerless to change the way things are; in *The Dynasts* the Shade of the Earth calls her

> Dame Nature—that lay-shape
> They use to hang phenomena upon—
> Whose deftest mothering in fairest spheres
> Is girt about by terms inexorable!
>
> (I, I, 6)

But these private personifications did not provide in themselves a system expansive enough to perform the functions of the supernatural element in an epic. Hardy had still to create the vast metaphorical structure in which he embodied their separate meanings. By 1886 he had solved his problem; in that year he entered in his notebook the two ideas which form the framework of *The Dynasts* and give symbolic form to the philosophical content:

The human race to be shown as one great network of tissue which quivers in every part when one point is shaken, like a spider's web if touched. Abstract realisms to be in the form of Spirits, Spectral figures, etc.

The Realities to be the true realities of life, hitherto called abstractions. The old material realities to be placed behind the former, as shadowy accessories (*Early Life,* p. 232).

The idea of intervolved humanity, and the idea that reality is an attribute of the Spirit-world, defined the structure of the epic; Hardy had only to turn the scheme into a poem.

The organizing principle of this vast scheme remains essentially that of the lyrics—an antinomial juxtaposition of the apparent (human individuality and free will) and "the true realities of life." As in many of the lyrics, the spirit world has more reality, more specificity, than the human one. The major spirits—the Spirit of the Years, the Spirit of the Pities, the Spirits Ironic and Sinister—maintain their individuality throughout the piece, while men are submerged into the vast, blurring symbols of brain and nerves, which are intended to exhibit "as one organism the anatomy of life and movement in all humanity and vitalized matter" (*Dynasts,* I, Fore Scene).

The use of a single symbol for all of mankind, and Hardy's constant insistence on the mechanistic nature of human actions, gives to the human actors an almost allegorical quality, as though each individual man were merely another manifestation of the abstraction, Humanity. Hardy supports this view of his human figures with his suggestion, in the Preface, that they assume

> a monotonic delivery of speeches, with dreamy conventional gestures, something in the manner traditionally maintained by the old Christmas mummers, the curiously hypnotizing impressiveness of whose automatic style—that of persons who spoke by no will of their own—may be remembered by all who ever experienced it (p. xi).

The most realistic human characters are generally anonymous—the men in the streets, the deserters, the harlots, the camp followers—characters who are simply called "A Spectator" or "Third Woman." Such characters often have highly individualized scenes, but because they are anonymous, and because their responses to events, though vigorous, are uncomprehending and ineffectual, they do not sustain their individuality, but flow together into one stream of the "brain-like network of currents and ejections" which is the controlling Immanent Will. The Dynasts are less individualized, perhaps because they are seen in more public, less personal, circumstances; one general speaks and acts much like another, and the Parliamentary debates might well be the speeches of one rather dull M.P.

The spirit-personalities, on the other hand, are developed in some detail, particularly the three—the Spirit of the Years, the Spirit of the Pities, and the Spirit Ironic—who compose the principal antinomial pattern of the Overworld. The Spirit of the Years is, as he says, "unpassioned"; he is the eldest spirit, and age has brought resignation and acceptance of the immutable. The Spirit of the Pities is the youngest spirit, "a mere juvenile," says the Spirit Ironic, "who only came into being in what the earthlings call their Tertiary Age." His speeches are consistently compassionate of human suffering, and he emotionally resists the cold wisdom of the Years. The Spirit Ironic, like the Spirit of the Pities, speaks with a human voice, that is he expresses a human, emotional response to the inexorable Will; but because he is older, his response is ironic, not pitying. These three voices are always easily distinguishable from each other, and the attitudes which they express are clear and consistent.

By thus humanizing his abstractions and abstracting his humans, Hardy gives unity to an otherwise hopelessly diverse chronicle. And, more important to the philosophic aim, he forces upon the reader the central ironic point. The Spirits, he says, are "the true realities of life"; it is the ironic relation of their comments to the action, rather than the action itself, which dominates the poem and points the meaning.

They thus provided Hardy with an opportunity which the lyrics, by their very nature, denied him—an opportunity to express his complex emotional response to the destinies of men in terms adequate to its complexity.

The two worlds of *The Dynasts,* and the interrelations within each and between the two, provide antinomial possibilities beyond any previous form that Hardy had tried. The principal opposition is drawn between earth and the Overworld, or more precisely between the degree of awareness possible to each. Humankind are, as the Spirits never tire of observing, automatons, and as such are incapable of seeing the reality in which they are entrapped. It is only the Spirits who can recognize

> the intolerable antilogy
> Of making figments feel,
>
> (I, IV, 6)

which is Hardy's basic perception of the human condition.

On earth and in the Overworld, further complicating contrasts exist. Since men are blind to their mechanistic state, earthly antinomies take the form of dramatic ironies: a French streetwalker chants "*Jubilate* like the rest," ignorant of France's defeat at Trafalgar; King George blandly denies Pitt's need of aid and hastens his death; generals see victory in defeat and defeat in victory. Usually Hardy, who was not one to let an irony go unnoticed, underscores these points by inserting commentaries by the Spirit Ironic, the Spirit Sinister, or the Spirit of Rumour.

In the Overworld there are also oppositions. Different spirit-groups express different, often contradictory, attitudes toward the human events below them—pity or ironic amusement or sinister delight or the philosophic resignation of the convinced determinist. The Spirits never alter their views and are never reconciled to each other; they cannot be, since, as the Spirit of the Years teaches his fellow spirits,

> We are in Its hand . . . Here, as elsewhere,
> We do but as we may; no further dare.
>
> (I, II, 2)

In short, on earth and in the Overworld alike, the organizing principle is that eternal, irreconcilable conflict which was for Hardy the first (and only) principle of existence—the disparity between the way things ought to be (and often for men *seem* to be) and the way things are.

To say that the Spirits can see the way things are is not to say that they are real, even symbolically—Hardy is not asserting that such supernatural consciousnesses exist. The Spirits rather represent the ways in which man, if he were completely conscious of his place in the universe, might respond. Hardy was rigorously faithful to his monistic vision. In the Preface to *The Dynasts,* he writes: "The wide prevalence of the Monistic theory of the Universe forbade, in this twentieth century, the importation of Divine personages from any antique Mythology as ready-made sources or channels of Causation, even in verse," and he urges the reader to take the Spirits "for what they may be worth as contrivances of the fancy merely" (p. viii). The Spirits express the way things are, as ignorant man cannot, but they do not exist as forces—the universe of *The Dynasts,* like the universe of the shorter poems, is a monistic one, in which the only operative force is a non-teleological energy called The Immanent Will. The world is still, as Hardy says in the Preface, "unintelligible."

The central opposition set up in *The Dynasts* between the earth and the Overworld in terms of the awareness possible to each corresponds roughly to the dark and light worlds of the lyrics, and is supported, as in the lyrics, by diction and imagery. *The Dynasts* is Hardy's major *tour de force* in diction, as it is in other qualities. The metaphor on which he built his epic drama provided him with two groups of speaking voices which correspond to the two kinds of language which he set up in his diagram of diction: the Spirits of the Overworld employ poetic diction, while humanity speaks the language of common speech. This division, which is maintained meticulously throughout the drama's 19 acts and 130 scenes, gives verbal consistency and unity to each world; it also establishes diction as a symbolic extension of the philosophical distinction between the two worlds. The Spirits speak a rich private language which is as different as possible from common speech, which is not even quite English. The "Persons" in the drama, on the other hand, speak two varieties of common speech: one for the "Dynasts," the other for the people.

The dynasts speak in flat, formalized standard English, the result in part of Hardy's scrupulous fidelity to his sources—Hansard for the Parliament scenes,[56] and a mass of histories, biographies, and memoirs for the rest. He wrote in his Preface to *The Dynasts* that ". . .whenever any evidence of the words really spoken or written by the characters in their various situations was attainable, as close a paraphrase has been aimed at as was compatible with the form chosen" (p. viii). The notes scattered through the text show that, even in translating from the French, Hardy strove above all for a close paraphrase. The common people speak, as one might expect, a more colloquial English which is, in the Wessex scenes, enriched with dialectal and archaic forms. It remains plain, however, and free of Hardy's personal eccentricities of diction—it is closer to the style of the novels than to that of the poems.

Any scene from the Overworld set against any one from the world of men will show how distinct, how diametrically opposed the two styles of diction are. The Fore Scene of Part First is typical of the Overworld style. It is highly stylized, complex in syntax, polysyllabic and abstract in vocabulary, full of coinages; it bears the mark of Hardy's personality and thought in every line. It is packed with the language of mechanistic action (*rapt aesthetic rote, automatic, unweeting, pulsion of the Byss, clock-like laws, engines*) and of biology (*animalcula, fibrils, veins, tissues, nerves, pulses, lobule*); the latter introduces the biological image of men and things as a single organism exhibiting "the anatomy of life and movement in all humanity and vitalized matter" which recurs throughout the drama—an image of life as simply another kind of machine. In the Spirit scenes Hardy also used personal coinages and rare and obsolete words more freely than in even the most idiosyncratic poems —*pulsion, Byss, warefulness, closelier, reflexed, wareness* occur in the Fore Scene.

Any of the earth scenes will do for a comparison. The prose scenes of Wessex life show Hardy's command of local dialect, and sometimes also his talent for folk humor, though the humor is often more literary than local, more Shakespeare's Warwickshire than Hardy's, or George the Third's, Dorset. The Shakespearian influence is more apparent in the blank verse of the dynastic scenes, which is rarely very effective poetry, and is at its worst either turgid and pompous or simply lamely pedestrian. This exchange from the fourth act of Part First is typical, though far from the worst:

KING
And now he has left Boulogne with all his host?
Was it his object to invade at all,
Or was his vast assemblage there a blind?

PITT
Undoubtedly he meant invasion, sir,
Had fortune favoured. He may try it yet.
And, as I said, could we but close with Fox. . . .

(I, IV, 1)

The diction of these scenes is standard, undistinguished, and undistinguishable—all human characters speak in pretty much the same formal style. The device of setting this style in contrast to its opposite—the flat, unvarying speech of the blind leaders of humanity against the rich and various language of the omniscient Overworld—supports the antinomial, ironic view of events which is at the heart of *The Dynasts*.

The imagery of *The Dynasts* works in much the same systematic way to strengthen the central opposition between what men see, and what they would see if they were truly conscious. Men speak without metaphor, because their vision is a vision of things-as-things, and not as relationships. Metaphor is a mode of knowing, and since man cannot know, he can speak only in flat, discursive, unmetaphorical language. Knowledge belongs to the Overworld, to ideal consciousness, and so does metaphor and imagery. In *The Dynasts* Men describe; Spirits relate.

The scenes involving men are consequently rapid, strenuously active, and often highly dramatic, but they are poetically flat; in these qualities they demonstrate Hardy's view of man's fate—to be active, but ignorant. The speeches of men are expository and factual—they provide detail, but not meaning; frequently Hardy dispenses with human speech altogether, showing men's actions in dumb show, which becomes a kind of metaphor in itself of the limits of man's awareness.

The speeches of the Overworld figures, on the other hand, are rich in imagery, and this richness is primarily a function of the principal advantage which the Spirits have over mankind—a long-range perspective. The Spirits can see as whole the movements which men see as separate—armies clashing, navies maneuvering, populations fleeing. This panoramic view is in turn a symbol of their philosophical perspective, which is the main point. This is made clear in the stage directions which set up the cosmic structure of the poem in the Fore Scene: from the Overworld,

Europe is disclosed as a prone and emaciated figure, the Alps shaping like a backbone, and the branching mountain-chains like ribs, the peninsular plateau of Spain forming a head,

and men and things can be seen

with a seeming transparency . . . exhibiting as one organism the anatomy of life and movement in all humanity and vitalized matter. . . .

What the Spirits see here is the Immanent Will, that encompassing energy which determines all actions of "men and things." These two images—the emaciated figure of Europe and the anatomy of life—are the key images of *The Dynasts*; the subsequent action is simply a vast explication of the meanings implicit in them. Perspective is what men do not and cannot have, and so the lofty vision of the Overworld provides both an expansive perspective of vast "epic" actions, and an ironically contracting philosophical perspective of what those actions mean.

The conflicts in the Overworld, I have said, are unresolved. They are unresolved because individually the Spirits express conflicting aspects of Hardy's own attitudes toward experience—the endless, wrangling debate they carry on mirrors the state of Hardy's mind throughout his life. By separating his conflicting views Hardy was able to make his philosophical difficulties dramatic, and to avoid the confusion and inconsistency which mar philosophical lyrics like "The Sleep-Worker." But the difficulties remain, and compose the philosophical structure of the poem.

The most basic and recurrent conflict in the Overworld is that set up so clearly in "The Convergence of the Twain," between "human" aspirations and emotions on the one hand, and the blind mechanism of the Immanent Will on the other. The Immanent Will is not present in the action; or, to be more precise, it *is* the action, as we see it in the following stage direction:

> The scene assumes the preternatural transparency before mentioned, and there is again beheld as it were the interior of a brain which seems to manifest the volitions of a Universal Will, of whose tissues the personages of the action form portion (I, I, 6).

The spokesman for this "Universal Will" is the Spirit of the Years, an unemotional voice of the wisdom of experience, who laments nothing, hopes for nothing, and makes no teleological concessions. He argues throughout the poem the "Inadvertent Mind," and his last judgment of the drama of Napoleon is as relentlessly mechanistic as his first utterance:

> Thus doth the Great Foresightless mechanize
> In blank entrancement now as evermore
> Its ceaseless artistries in Circumstance ....
>
> (III, After Scene)

He speaks for the rationalistic side of Hardy's mind, the side which could not be content with anything less than a full look at the worst.

At the other pole of the antinomy stand the Spirit of the Pities and its Chorus, expressing Hardy's compassion and deep humanity. The group approximates, Hardy says in his Preface,

'the Universal Sympathy of human nature—the spectator idealized' of the Greek Chorus; it is impressionable and inconsistent in its views, which sway hither and thither as wrought on by events (p. ix).

Pity is a rather inadequate term to describe this universal sympathy; Charity (in Saint Paul's sense) might be better, or simply Love.

The relation of the Pities to the Years is roughly that of an advocate before a justice (in which case the Immanent Will is the Law). Thus at Austerlitz the Pities plead their case:

> O Great Necessitator, heed us now!
> If it indeed must be
> That this day Austria smoke with slaughtery,
> Quicken the issue as Thou knowest how;
> And dull to suffering those whom it befalls
> To quit their lodgment in a flesh that galls!

and the Years replies:

> Again ye deprecate the World-Soul's way
> That I so long have told? Then note anew
> (Since ye forget) the ordered potencies,
> Nerves, sinews, trajects, eddies, ducts of It
> The Eternal Urger, pressing change on change,
>
> (I, VI, 3)

and we see once more the vision of mankind as the entangled network of a great, twitching brain. The plea has been thrown out of court.

The relation of Pities and Years is generally one of appeal and denial, or of question and answer (many of their exchanges are in the form of a catechism), and this is an appropriate relationship for the thesis and antithesis in an antinomial pattern. There is, however, one other important voice—that of the Spirit Ironic. In the Austerlitz scene, it is the Semichorus of Ironic Spirits who explicate to the Pities the vision of the great brain:

> O Innocents, can ye forget
> That things to be were shaped and set
> Ere mortals and this planet met?

They go on to summarize Hardy's view of evolution, describing how, in the past, they

> Beheld the rarest wrecked amain,
> Whole nigh-perfected species slain
> By those that scarce could boast a brain;
>
> Saw ravage, growth, diminish, add,
> Here peoples sane, there peoples mad,
> In choiceless throws of good and bad;
>
> Heard laughters at the ruthless dooms
> Which tortured to the eternal glooms
> Quick, quivering hearts in hecatombs.
>
> (I, VI, 3)

This sounds at first like more of the bleak mechanism of the Spirit of the Years; but in fact it is very different in tone. The Ironic Spirits accept the wisdom of the Years, but their response to it is as emotional as is that of the Pities; the account may be evolutionary, but the language is scarcely scientific or objective ("ravaged," "mad," "tortured," "quivering hearts"). For Hardy irony and pity, like tragedy and comedy, are simply alternate ways of responding to circumstance; and in fact the Pities do describe human life as tragedy, while the Ironic Spirits see it as comedy. Both of these responses are abundantly present in the lyric poems as well as in *The Dynasts,* and it would scarcely be an exaggeration to say that they were the only responses to experience available to Hardy. Those poems of which we are fondest are probably poems of the Pities, but there are plenty of Ironic poems as well: the "Satires of Circumstance," for example, are in this tone, and the Ancient Briton in "The Moth-Signal" is a grinning Ironic Spirit. The streak of cruelty which runs through the poems, in which Hardy seems almost to rejoice in the inevitable defeat of human fortunes, takes systematic form in *The Dynasts* as the Spirit Ironic. It is the other side of Pity, the reaction to suffering of a man who feels it too much.

It is the Pities who have the last speech:

> But—a stirring thrills the air
> Like to sounds of joyance there
>   That the rages
>   Of the ages
> Shall be cancelled, and deliverance offered from the darts
>   that were,
> Consciousness the Will informing, till It fashion all
>   things fair!
>
> (III, After Scene)

This final burst of "evolutionary meliorism" has seemed to some critics a contradiction of Hardy's pessimism, and a flaw in the poem as a whole, which should not be taken seriously. Nevertheless, there the speech is, and in a position which prevents our ignoring it; we *must* take it seriously if we take any of the poem seriously.

It is true that the final speech cannot be reconciled with a philosophy of unmitigated pessimism; but to see Hardy's thought as simply that is to miss completely the significance of his antinomial patterns, and to read into his thought a finality and a consistency which are not there. The Pities, as I have said, represent a deep compassion which is an essential part of Hardy's attitude toward existence, though it cannot easily be reconciled with the absolute determinism which the concept of the Immanent Will implies. But the point of *The Dynasts,* and of Hardy's philosophical verse in general, is not that the determinism of the Immanent Will is true and the human sympathy of the Pities sentimental and false. The Pities express, as Hardy says, the "Universal Sympathy of human nature"; while man endures, their attitude will be a valid one. The dialectic of *The Dynasts* is between these two attitudes; neither is urged as the whole truth, for though determinism may have all the evidence on its side, hope and compassion are inherent in human nature, and cannot be denied. Hardy's reason told him that man's fate was determined; yet he could urge man to face

> The fact of life with dependence placed
> On the human heart's resource alone,
> In brotherhood bonded close and graced
>
> With loving-kindness fully blown,
> And visioned help unsought, unknown.
>
> (*Collected Poems,* p. 306)

"Loving-kindness" is not from the vocabulary of determinism, but it is a common term in Hardy's poetry, and one must take it into account in considering the philosophical meaning of the poems, particularly of *The Dynasts*.

The Dynasts poses a philosophical problem—how can determinism and man's consciousness of injustice be reconciled?—but it offers no solution; the Pities have the final speech, but the speech is not a resolution. "Yes," Hardy wrote to his friend Clodd, "I left off on a note of hope. It was just as well that the Pities should have the last word, since, like *Paradise Lost, The Dynasts* proves nothing" (*Later Years*, p. 276).

Hardy is not quite right. Philosophically, *The Dynasts* does not prove anything: it is not in the nature of poetry to provide such proof. But technically, *The Dynasts* proves a good deal about Hardy as a poet. It proves, first of all, that Hardy could make his antinomial vision do the structural work of more involved and more consistent beliefs, in holding a complex poetic form together, but that he could not make a philosophy out of it; the ideas function in *The Dynasts* not as a system, but as the elements in that cosmic irony which was as close as he ever got to an answer. It proves, further, that his idiosyncratic patterns of diction and imagery could be made to function on a large scale, and with some delicacy of discrimination—that he could make odd words and odd perspectives seem necessary.

The Dynasts is not essentially different, either in thought or in style, from characteristic early lyrics—once again, development is not a valid consideration here. Rather it is a vast testing ground on which Hardy could discover the range and the limits of that thought and that style, and the right relationship between them. But, more than that, *The Dynasts* is a modern epic that works. In belongs among the great eccentric works of our time, and its greatness justifies its eccentricity.

10

The Final Achievement

A FEW WEEKS before his death, Hardy told his wife that "he had done all that he meant to do, but he did not know whether it had been worth doing" (*Later Years,* p. 263). In this remark, Hardy made two related judgments of his own achievement, neither of which is what one would expect of a major artist, though both are characteristic, and revealing, of Hardy. First, the sense of fulfilled intention is unusual; Conrad's judgment of his achievement in *Nostromo* is much more typical of an artist's attitude toward his completed work: "Personally," Conrad wrote, "I am not satisfied. It is something—but not *the* thing I tried for."[57] Hardy did not seem to feel this very common sense of disparity between intention and performance—his work apparently *was* the thing he tried for. (This lack of artistic discontent may help to explain the presence in the *Collected Poems* of so many unsuccessful poems, and also Hardy's failure to develop artistically.) Second, the doubt as to the value of what he had done: this seems less a question of the value of his specific writings than a doubt as to the value of art in general—is it *ever* worth doing? Surely few artists would devote their lives so wholeheartedly to a vocation about which they entertained such fundamental doubts.

Both points are entirely characteristic of Hardy, and the whole remark is very much in the voice of the Old Stoic, who speaks so frequently in the poems, particularly in the later ones. In "He Never Expected Much," a poem from the posthumous *Winter Words,* the world tells the speaker:

> "I do not promise overmuch,
>   Child; overmuch;
> Just neutral-tinted haps and such". . .

and the speaker accepts this "wise warning,"

> And hence could stem such strain and ache
>   As each year might assign.
>
>   (*Winter Words,* pp. 113-14)

Hardy seems to have carried this stoic acceptance of limitation over into his aesthetic judgments. He "never expected much" of his gifts, and he made no claims for the power of poetry or for the peculiar wisdom and importance of the poet. Poetry was for him a means of exploring reality, but he did not distinguish it from other possible means such as philosophy and religion; "poetry and religion," he wrote, "touch each other, or rather modulate into each other" (*Collected Poems,* p. 530). Poetry was simply another human activity, no more likely to succeed or to impress itself upon the Immanent Will than any other of man's actions.

This quality of undemanding, resigned endurance dominates Hardy's work, and it is no doubt for this reason that our final impression of the poems is rather an impression of an attitude than of an art; we discover and admire the man, but we miss or undervalue the pattern which he has made of his beliefs. Surely the man we discover is an impressive figure—a man of inflexible integrity who saw the world as a tragic irony at humanity's expense, and who tried to make his poetry the direct and honest mirror of that vision. This personality, for all Hardy's reticence and Victorian decorum, dominates the poems and makes them, as we become familiar with their private eloquence, a single personal testament.

But we should also be aware of another aspect of the man—of Hardy the craftsman, the dedicated poet. For Hardy was as true to his craft, as he understood it, as he was to his ironic vision of the world; and we do him a great injustice if, in responding to his humanity, we fail to recognize his conscientious and meticulous craftsmanship.

We are hampered in this recognition by the fact that Hardy's artistic fidelities were eccentric, and that his standards of poetic excellence were often not traditional standards. Examining the elements which go to make up Hardy's poetry—the ponderous, ill-conceived philosophy, the gabble of mixed diction, the quirkish stanza forms, the obsessive images and situations—one is moved to conclude of each that it will not do, that this is not the stuff of which great poetry is made. Yet Hardy contrived to make it do, and to make himself a major poet.

Often the good poems exist in a perilous balance of these ungainly elements, and many of the others fail to maintain that balance. Because the elements are so eccentric, the balance, when it is maintained, is an admirable, even astonishing thing, and we may admire it simply as a curious feat, as we would a juggling trick. When it is not maintained, we may think, "small wonder," and forgive or dismiss Hardy according to the degree of our tolerance of failure.

But we should recognize that Hardy's eccentricities are all of a piece, that they are interrelated and mutually supporting; language and metrics are the products of each other, the imagery derives from the philosophy, and all the elements together compose the pattern of antinomies which I have suggested is Hardy's principal structural device. It is important to recognize the consistency of the poems as a whole—a consistency of tone and manner and point of view which overshadows the small, particular inconsistencies of thought of which Hardy was occasionally guilty. The essential consistency may be obscured to the critic by the fact that it sometimes led Hardy to violations of taste and convention, and produced poems which are at best curious failures; but this shows only that the consistent, ironic instrument was not sufficiently adjustable to the range of particular poetic events against which Hardy directed it. The consistency remains, and it remains as a virtue of the poems, for if it sometimes led Hardy astray, it also led him, perhaps unconsciously, to poetic effects which are dramatically successful.

As a poet, Hardy worked under severe limitations—some the limitations of his time, some of his own nature, some of his circumstances. His age offered him both an unwieldy mass of thought to absorb his mind and a public radically hostile to that thought. His relatively untrained mind accepted uncritically the current ideas of his time, and never succeeded in reducing them to a coherent system. His circumstances forced him into thirty years of writing fiction before he could turn his undivided attention to poetry. Yet he confronted these limitations, and struggled with them to develop a style which would say what he felt compelled to say, in poetry of his own choosing, in his own voice.

Because of his limitations it seems safe to say that Hardy left a larger body of unsuccessful verse than any other major poet of the English language. His art was crippled partly by the ideas he forced into it, and partly by technical limitations. Like Hopkins, he found the inherited conventions of his craft inadequate to his needs, but, unlike Hopkins, he did not have the peculiar kind of creative genius which could leave conventions alone and start over. He went on using them intermittently—the conventional meters, the conventional modes of diction—though he tried to adapt them to his own necessities. Because his critical sense was undeveloped and fallible, his efforts were not always successful, and he was slow to recognize his failures.

Yet there remains a core of fine poetry, which rises above the philosophy and the conventions, which makes fresh poetic use of the eccentricities of style, and which succeeds in expressing Hardy's world in the precise, meticulous perceptions of a sensitive and humble man. That world is a narrow and incomplete one—dark, melancholy, retrospective —a world without joy, in which hope is a snare and love a catastrophe. Hardy argued the necessity of "a full look at the Worst," and he took that look without flinching. Perhaps in the intensity of his looking he missed much that we may think good, and worth seeing; yet within the limits of his perceptions, his vision was clear. His expressed certain themes—mutability and the passing of time, mortality, the courage of stoicism—in poems which are honest, moving, and uniquely personal. He was a pessimist, but his was not often the sentimental pessimism of Housman: not "I a stranger and afraid/In a world I never made," but "I never cared for Life: Life cared for me,/And hence I owed it some fidelity" (*Collected Poems,* p. 657).

In the end, it is that fidelity to Life which is at the heart of Hardy's greatness. He found a world which was indifferent to human suffering, hostile to man's highest aspirations, compounded of violence and unreason, "cramped by crookedness, custom, and fear"— a world in which man seemed to survive best by self-delusion; he denied himself the comfort of that delusion, looked calmly and steadily at reality, and tried to write what he saw. What he saw was fortunately not a world of philosophical abstractions, but the world around him, colored by his own ideas and his own imagination. He put it into the poems as he saw it—a world of commonplaces clearly seen, of "the other side of common emotions," of microcosmic detail, set in the profoundly personal idiom of the perceiver. Fidelity to life in such terms is a high poetic achievement.

References and Notes

References

References to Hardy's works are to the following editions:

Collected Novels and Stories, London, Macmillan & Co., Ltd., 1951, 18 vols.

Collected Poems, New York, The Macmillan Company, 1948.

The Dynasts: A Drama of the Napoleonic Wars, in Three Parts, Nineteen Acts, & One Hundred and Thirty Scenes. Part First, London, Macmillan & Co., Ltd., New York, The Macmillan Company, 1903. Part Second, London and New York, 1905. Part Third, London, Macmillan & Co., Ltd., 1908.

The Famous Tragedy of the Queen of Cornwall, London, Macmillan & Co., Ltd., 1923.

Human Shows, Far Phantasies, Songs, and Trifles, London, Macmillan, & Co., Ltd., 1925.

Late Lyrics and Earlier, London, Macmillan & Co., Ltd., 1922.

Life and Art, edited by Ernest Brennecke, Jr., New York, Greenberg, 1925.

Moments of Vision and Miscellaneous Verses, London, Macmillan & Co., Ltd., 1917.

Poems of the Past and the Present, London and New York, Harper & Bros., 1902.

Satires of Circumstance, London, Macmillan & Co., Ltd., 1914.

Selected Poems of Thomas Hardy, London, Macmillan & Co., Ltd., 1916.

Selected Poems of William Barnes, Chosen and Edited with a Preface and Glossarial Notes by Thomas Hardy, London, Henry Frowde, 1908.

Time's Laughingstocks and Other Verses, London, Macmillan and Co., Ltd., 1909.

Wessex Poems and Other Verses, London and New York, Harper and Bros., 1898.

Winter Words in Various Moods and Metres, London, Macmillan & Co., Ltd., 1928.

References concerning Hardy's biography are from the two volumes published by Mrs. Florence Emily Hardy:

The Early Life of Thomas Hardy, New York, The Macmillan Company, 1928.

The Later Years of Thomas Hardy, New York, The Macmillan Company, 1930.

Notes

1. In *Friends of a Lifetime: Letters to Sydney Carlyle Cockerell*, edited by Viola Meynell (London: Jonathan Cape, 1940), p. 297.
2. Cf. Ernest Brennecke, Jr., *Thomas Hardy's Universe: A Study of a Poet's Mind* (London: T. Fisher Unwin, 1924); W. R. Rutland, *Thomas Hardy: A Study of His Writings and Their Background* (Oxford: Basil Blackwell, 1938); Harvey Curtis Webster, *On a Darkling Plain: The Art and Thought of Thomas Hardy* (Chicago: University of Chicago Press, 1947); also Joseph Warren Beach, *The Concept of Nature in Nineteenth-Century English Poetry* (New York: The Macmillan Company, 1936); John Holloway, *The Victorian Sage* (London: Macmillan & Co., Ltd., 1953); and essays by Howard Baker, Jacques Barzun, Delmore Schwartz, and Allen Tate in *The Southern Review*, VI (Summer, 1940).
3. Hardy's complete notebooks have not, of course, been published. When I refer to "the notebooks" I generally mean those portions of his notes which were transcribed in Mrs. Hardy's two volumes of biography. The disconnected notes from three previously unpublished notebooks which Evelyn Hardy has published as *Thomas Hardy's Notebooks* (London: Hogarth Press, 1955) add virtually nothing of importance to our knowledge of Hardy; they are in the same vein as the notes quoted by Mrs. Hardy, and support the same generalizations.
4. Quoted in C. Day Lewis, "The Lyrical Poetry of Thomas Hardy," *Proceedings of the British Academy*, XXXVII (1953), 164.
5. *Ibid.*, p. 174; John Crowe Ransom, "Honey and Gall," *The Southern Review*, VI (Summer, 1940), 4.
6. In a letter in response to a friendly review of *Jude*, Hardy wrote: "If I say to a lady 'I met a naked woman', it is indelicate. But if I go on to say 'I found she was mad with sorrow', it ceases to be indelicate. And in writing *Jude* my mind was fixed on the ending" (*Later Years*, p. 43). And in *The Flurried Years* (London: Hurst and Blackett, Ltd., no date) Violet Hunt records Hardy's account of a recurrent dream: "I am pursued, and I am rising like an angel up into heaven, out of the hands of my earthly pursuers. . . . I am agitated and hampered, as I suppose an angel would not be, by—a paucity of underlinen" (p. 69).
7. *Thomas Hardy: A Study of the Wessex Novels, The Poems, and The Dynasts* (Manchester, University Press, 1937), p. 347.
8. *Thomas Hardy: A Study of His Writings and Their Background*, p. 264.

9. In the thirty-odd years since Hardy's death, two books on *The Dynasts* and one on the poetry have appeared. Both studies of *The Dynasts*—Amiya Chakravarty's *The Dynasts and the Post-War Age in Poetry* (London, New York, Toronto: Oxford University Press, 1938) and J. O. Bailey's *Thomas Hardy and the Cosmic Mind* (Chapel Hill: The University of North Carolina Press, 1956)—are primarily concerned with Hardy's ideas, and neither gives much attention to the poetry as such. James Granville Southworth's *The Poetry of Thomas Hardy* (New York: Columbia University Press, 1947) does, insofar as it classifies the principal themes and techniques in the poems, but it does not go very far toward relating the two.

10. *ABC of Reading* (London: Faber and Faber, 1951), p. 193.

11. *Friends of a Lifetime*, p. 290.

12. G. K. Chesterton, *The Victorian Age in Literature* (New York: Henry Holt, 1913), p. 143.

13. *Mightier Than the Sword* (London: George Allen & Unwin, 1938), p. 142.

14. Quoted in Ernest Brennecke, Jr., *The Life of Thomas Hardy* (New York, Greenberg, 1925), p. 5.

15. These are listed in Appendices 5, 6, and 10 of Carl J. Weber's *Hardy of Wessex: His Life and Literary Career* (New York: Columbia University Press, 1940).

16. Hardy does mention that he read and disliked James's *The Reverberator* (*Early Life*, p. 277); elsewhere he describes James as "the Polonius of novelists" (*Later Years*, pp. 7-8).

17. Quoted in Basil Champneys, *Memoirs and Correspondence of Coventry Patmore* (London: George Bell & Sons, 1912), II, 262-63.

18. *Further Letters of Gerard Manley Hopkins* (London: Oxford University Press, 1938), p. 222.

19. "A Modern Classic, William Barnes," in *Principle in Art* (London: George Bell & Sons, 1912), p. 139.

20. "Thoughts on Beauty and Art," *Macmillan's Magazine*, IV (May-Oct. 1861), 133.

21. *Further Letters*, p. 222.

22. "Poetry and Propaganda," *The Bookman*, LXX (Feb. 1930), 597.

23. *Autobiographies* (London: Macmillan & Co., Ltd., 1955), p. 115.

24. Hardy confessed to William Archer that, ". . . if belief were a matter of choice, I should prefer to accept the spiritual hypothesis," and added: "The material world is so uninteresting, human life is so miserably bounded, circumscribed, cabin'd, cribb'd, confined. I want another domain for the imagination to expatiate in." Archer, *Real Conversations* (London: W. Heinemann, 1904), pp. 44-45.

25. Quoted in Alfred Noyes, *Two Worlds for Memory* (London and New York: Sheed and Ward, 1953), p. 147.

26. *Thomas Hardy: The Novels and Stories* (Cambridge: Harvard University Press, 1949), p. 7.

27. *Real Conversations*, p. 45.

28. "Honey and Gall," *The Southern Review*, VI (Summer, 1940), 7.

29. *Language as Gesture* (New York: Harcourt, Brace and Company, 1952), p. 79.

30. W. Somerset Maugham, *Cakes and Ale* (Garden City: Doubleday, Doran & Co., 1930), pp. 134-35.

31. "Mr. Hardy's New Poems," *New Statesman*, IV (Dec. 19, 1914), 270;

reprinted in Strachey, *Characters and Commentaries* (New York: Harcourt, Brace and Company, 1933), p. 182.

32. *Spectator* (April 5, 1902), 517; *Saturday Review*, XCIII (Jan. 11, 1902), 49.

33. Coventry Patmore, *Amelia, Tamerton Church-Tower, Etc.*, with Prefatory Study on English Metrical Law (London: George Bell & Sons, 1878), p. 12.

34. These are catalogued in an appendix to Elizabeth Cathcart Hickson's *The Versification of Thomas Hardy* (Philadelphia: University of Pennsylvania Press, 1931), pp. 120-27.

35. Edmund Gosse, "The Lyrical Poetry of Thomas Hardy," in *Some Diversions of a Man of Letters* (New York: Charles Scribner's Sons, 1919), p. 245. For a catalogue of these inventions, see Hickson, *The Versification of Thomas Hardy*, pp. 92-119.

36. John Hollander, "The Metrical Emblem," *Kenyon Review*, XXI (Spring, 1959), 282.

37. *Mightier Than the Sword*, p. 143.

38. Letter to *Times Literary Supplement*, no. 108 (Feb. 5, 1904), 36-37.

39. *Poems* (London: Oxford University Press, 1948), p. 9.

40. Edmund Blunden, *Thomas Hardy* (London: Macmillan and Co., 1942), p. 165.

41. *Autobiographies*, p. 142.

42. *The Letters of Henry James*, edited by Lubbock (New York: Charles Scribner's Sons, 1920), I, 200.

43. Quoted in Blunden, *Thomas Hardy*, pp. 56-57.

44. *TLS*, no. 214 (Feb. 16, 1906), pp. 49-50.

45. "Hardy the Poet," *The Southern Review*, VI (Summer, 1940), 88.

46. *The Versification of Thomas Hardy*, pp. 120-27. Classification is based on that in the *NED*.

47. George G. Loane, "'The Dynasts' and the N. E. D.," (letter), *TLS*, no. 1, 411 (Feb. 14, 1929), 118.

48. Quoted in Blunden, *Thomas Hardy*, p. 104.

49. *Real Conversations*, p. 49.

50. Robert Graves, *Good-bye to All That* (London: Jonathan Cape, 1929), p. 374.

51. *Ibid.*, p. 376.

52. "Preface to the Second Edition of . . . 'Lyrical Ballads,'" *The Poetical Works of Wordsworth* (New York: Oxford University Press, 1950), p. 734.

53. In *Thomas Hardy's Notebooks*, p. 45, Evelyn Hardy quotes the following entry of March 13, 1874: "Let Europe be the stage and have scenes continually shifting." This may be, as Miss Hardy suggests, the first extant note relating to *The Dynasts*. Hardy himself was doubtful; many years later he added the query: "Can this refer to any conception of The Dynasts?"

54. I have used *poem* here in reference to *The Dynasts*, not because it is precisely accurate, but because there is no other generic term which is much better.

55. Hardy may have gotten the germ of this idea from Schlegel; on June 16, 1875, he wrote in his notebook: "Reading the Life of Goethe. Schlegel says that 'the deepest want and deficiency of all modern art lies

NOTES

in the fact that the artists have no mythology'" (*Thomas Hardy's Notebooks*, p. 51).

56. The scenes which take place in the House of Commons (Part I, Act I, Scene III and Part III, Act V, Scene V) are based on Hansard's *Parliamentary Debates*, and are frequently almost exact quotations. They are, however, considerably condensed; Part III, Act V, Scene V, a scene of some 200 lines in *The Dynasts*, is based on a 20,000 word debate (see *Parliamentary Debates*, First Series, vol. 30, cols. 417-63, "Address on the Prince Regent's Message relating to the Events in France"). Hardy is most meticulous when he is quoting petitions, amendments, and other verbatim statements. For example, Hansard quotes Castlereagh's motion:

"That an humble Address be presented to his royal highness the Prince Regent, to return to his Royal Highness the thanks of this House for his most gracious Message:

"To assure his Royal Highness, that it is impossible for his Majesty's faithful Commons not to be fully sensible of the dangers to which the tranquillity and independence of Europe are exposed in consequence of the events which have recently occurred in France, in direct contravention of the engagements concluded with the Allied Powers at Paris in the course of the last year:

"That, in a cause of such general concern, it must afford us the greatest satisfaction to learn that his Royal Highness has lost no time in entering into communications with his Majesty's Allies, for the purpose of forming such a concert as may most effectually provide for the general and permanent security of Europe.

"That, with a view to this important object, we shall, with the utmost zeal and alacrity, afford the requisite assistance to enable his Royal Highness to make an augmentation of his Majesty's forces by sea and land, and to adopt all such measures as may be necessary for its accomplishment" (Cols. 434-35).

Compare Hardy's version of the same speech in *The Dynasts*, III, V, 5.

57. Letter to William Rothenstein, in G. Jean-Aubry, *Joseph Conrad: Life and Letters* (Garden City: Doubleday, Page & Co., 1927), I, 336.

Index

Index

" 'According to the Mighty Working,' " 102-4
"Afterwards," 30, 124-26
"'ΑΓΝΩΣΤΩι ΘΕΩι," 37
" 'Ah, Are You Digging?' " 53-54
" 'And There Was a Great Calm,' " 105-7
"Apology," *Late Lyrics and Earlier*, 35, quoted, 176
Archer, William, 93
"Architectural Masks," 45
"At a Bridal," quoted, 57
"At Middle-field Gate in February," quoted, 120
"At Waking," 87
Auden, W. H., 34, 59, 73, 151

Barnes, William, 61, 102; influence on Hardy, 23-32; quoted, 30
"Before and After Summer," 46, 51
"Before Life and After," 51
"Before Marching and After," 51
"Bereft," 70-72, 87
Blackmur, R. P., quoted, 56
"Bride-Night Fire, The," 16, 25
Bridges, Robert, 21, 30, 79, 90
"Broken Appointment, A," 58-60, 66, 127
Browning, Robert, 21, 22, 27, 88

"Caged Goldfinch, The," quoted, 144
Cockerell, Sir Sydney, 8, 16, 17
"Come Not; Yet Come," 101
Conrad, Joseph, quoted, 175

"Convergence of the Twain, The," 46-48, 168
"Coquette and After, The," 46, 51
Crabbe, George, 110
"Curate's Kindness, The," 25

"Darkling Thrush, The," quoted, 113
"Days to Recollect," 101
Desperate Remedies, 14
"Domicilium," 130
Donne, John, 64
"Doom and She," 37
Duffin, H. C., 13
"During Wind and Rain," 115, 121-23, 149-50
Dynasts, The, 36, 91, 126, 132-33, 139, 146, 152-74; press reception of, 12, 91; Overworld in, 67, 161; experimental metrics in, 79-80; Hardy's defense of, 81-82; diction in, 92, 164-66; genesis of, 153-59; organization of, 160-63; imagery of, 166-67

Early Life of Thomas Hardy, The, composition of, 7-8
Eliot, T. S., 7, 49, 59, 60, 75, 79, 90, 151; on Hardy's philosophy, 34
English Review, 19

Famous Tragedy of the Queen of Cornwall, The, 155
Far from the Madding Crowd, 85

INDEX

Faulkner, William, 24
"Five Students, The," 53
Ford, Ford Madox, quoted, 18-19, 79

"God-Forgotten," 37
"God's Education," 36
Gosse, Edmund, 74-75
Graves, Robert, quoted, 102, 108
Guerard, Albert J., quoted, 43

"Hap," 67; quoted, 5, 158
Hardy, Emma Lavinia Gifford, 9, 153
Hardy, Florence Emily, 7, 20
Hardy, Thomas, Victorianism of, 10-11; attitude toward fiction, 17-19; debt to Barnes, 23-32; theory of evolution, 38, 111-12, 170; irony in, 41-55, 105-7; relation to ballad literature, 80-83; influence of popular music on, 83-85; debt to *New Version* (Tate and Brady), 85-88; influence of Old Testament, 117-19; revisions of poems, 139-50
"He Fears His Good Fortune," quoted, 51
"He Never Expected Much," quoted, 176
"Heiress and Architect," 53
"Her Apotheosis," quoted, 141-42
"Her Death and After," 51; quoted, 142-43
Hopkins, Gerard Manley, 21, 60, 75, 90; remarks on Barnes quoted, 28, 29, 30; compared to Hardy, 32-33, 73, 79, 179; "Author's Preface" to *Poems* quoted, 84
Housman, A. E., 13, 54, 179
Human Shows, 114, 140
Hymns Ancient and Modern, 87

"'I Have Lived with Shades,'" 87
"'If It's Ever Spring Again,'" 69-70
"In a Waiting-Room," quoted, 113
"In Tenebris," 61, 101; quoted, 121
"In the Days of Crinoline," 6
"In Time of 'The Breaking of Nations,'" 51; quoted, 104, 149
"Interloper, The," 97

James, Henry, Hardy compares to Meredith, 23; comment on *Tess* quoted, 91
"January Night, A," 62, 67
Job, Book of, 117-18
Johnson, Lionel, 12
Jude the Obscure, 12, 18, 133, 155; quoted, 43

"Lacking Sense, The," 112
"Lament of the Looking-Glass, The," 96
Laodicean, A, 133
"Last Signal, The," 24, 29
"Last Words to a Dumb Friend," 94
Late Lyrics and Earlier, 140
Later Years of Thomas Hardy, The, composition of, 7-8
Leavis, F. R., quoted on Hardy's diction, 91, 93
"Leipzig," 80
Life's Little Ironies, 81
"Lodging-House Fuchsias, The," 51-52
"Looking Across," 101
"Louisa in the Lane," 51

"Master and the Leaves, The," 92
Maugham, W. Somerset, quoted, 56
Mayor of Casterbridge, The, 14, 18, 86
"Memory and I," 53
Meredith, George, 22, 23, 30, 60, 90, 114
"Merrymaking in Question, A," 46, 127-28
"Midnight on the Great Western," 92
Moments of Vision, 132, 139, 140
Morgan, Charles, recalls Hardy at Oxford, 10, 12
Morris, William, 21, 89
"Moth-Signal, The," 147, 171
"Mother Mourns, The," 28, 37
Moule, Horace, 8
Murry, John Middleton, 12
"My Cicely," 14; quoted, 145-46

"Nature's Questioning," 36
"Near Lanivet, 1872," 118

INDEX 193

"Neutral Tones," 135-37, 139
New Version of the Psalms of David, A (Tate and Brady), 86-87
"New Year's Eve," 36
"Night in November, A," 8-10
Noyes, Alfred, 35-36, 41, 130

Oxford Book of Victorian Verse, 13

Pair of Blue Eyes, A, 43
"Paths of Former Time," quoted, 92
Patmore, Coventry, 21, 22, 28, 30, 60, 79, 83; Hardy's letter to, quoted, 23; admiration for Barnes, 29; relation to Hopkins and Hardy, 32; criticism of *Woodlanders*, 91
"Peasant's Confession, The," 80
Poems and Ballads (Swinburne), 22
Poems of Life in the Dorset Dialect (Barnes), 23
"Poems of 1912-13," 9, 24, 132, 137-38
"Poems of Pilgrimage," 132
Poems of the Past and the Present, 37, 132, 139, 140
Poor Man and the Lady, The, 16
Pound, Ezra, 15, 61, 75, 90; on Hardy's verse, quoted, 14
"Profitable Reading of Fiction, The," quoted, 64-65

"Quid Hic Agis?" 101

Ransom, John Crowe, quoted, 54
"Reminiscences of a Dancing Man," Ford on, 19
Return of the Native, The, 111, 128, 155
"Revulsion," 134-36, 139
"Roman Road, The," 128
Rutland, W. R., 13

"Sacrilege, The," 81
"San Sebastian," 80
"Satires of Circumstance" (group of poems), 45, 171
Satires of Circumstance (volume of poems), 131-32, 137, 139, 140
"Seeing the Moon Rise," 130

Selected Poems of William Barnes, Hardy's Preface to, quoted 24, 26-27, 28, 29, 31
Selected Poems of Thomas Hardy, 139
Shakespeare, William, 50, 59, 165
"Signs and Tokens," 67
"Singer Asleep, A," 22
"Sleep-Worker, The," 38, 168
"Spot, A," 87
Strachey, Lytton, 12; quoted, 57
"Subalterns, The," 37
"Sunday Morning Tragedy, A," 19, 81, 93
Swinburne, Algernon, 22

Tate and Brady. See *New Version of the Psalms of David*
Tennyson, Alfred, Lord, 23, 28
Tess of the D'Urbervilles, 18, 19, 42-43, 116, 133
Thomas, Dylan, 40, 73
Time's Laughingstocks, 85, 132, 139, 140, 146
"Timing Her," 85
"To Lizbie Brown," 101
"Trampwoman's Tragedy, A," 94
Trumpet Major, The, 25
Turner, J. M. W., Hardy's opinion of, 109

Under the Greenwood Tree, 83, 86
Untermeyer, Louis, 13
"Valenciennes," 25, 80
"Voice, The," 77-78, 137-39

Weber, Carl J., 8
Wessex Poems, 12, 20, 25, 77, 139, 140
"Wife in London, A," 43-45
Williams, William Carlos, 61
"Winter in Durnover Field," quoted, 116
Winter Words, 4, 131
Woolf, Virginia, 11
Wordsworth, William, 76, 89, 100, 150

Yeats, William Butler, 10, 11, 21, 49, 63, 75, 151; on loss of religion, 40; on William Morris, 89-90

www.ingramcontent.com/pod-product-compliance
Lightning Source LLC
Chambersburg PA
CBHW021405290426
44108CB00010B/398